40·40

A SHORT HISTORY OF EDUCATION IN JAMAICA

Millicent Whyte M.A. (Edn.) B.Sc. (Econ.)
Senior Lecturer
Mico Teachers' College
Jamaica

HODDER AND STOUGHTON
LONDON SYDNEY AUCKLAND TORONTO

British Library Cataloguing in Publication Data

Whyte, Millicent
A Short history of education in Jamaica.
—2nd ed.
1. Education—Jamaica—History
I. Title
370'.97292   LA496

ISBN 0 340 34318 4

First published 1977
Second edition 1983

Copyright © Millicent Whyte 1977 and 1983

All rights reserved. No part of this publication may be reproduced or transmitted in any form or by any means, electronic or mechanical, including photocopying, recording, or any information storage and retrieval system, without permission in writing from the publisher.

Printed in Great Britain for
Hodder and Stoughton Educational
a division of Hodder and Stoughton Ltd.,
Mill Road, Dunton Green, Sevenoaks, Kent
by Richard Clay (The Chaucer Press) Ltd, Bungay, Suffolk.

Foreword

To condense nearly a century and a half of educational history into so little space is a major undertaking. All the more so when, as in the present case, the corpus of materials into which a writer can dip is lacking neither in volume nor in significance. Mrs Whyte is, therefore, to be commended on producing this readable text.

As a lecturer in Education at Mico, her intention, I am sure, was principally to whet the appetite of training college students for the history of education as a means of illuminating other parts of the study of education. To this area of knowledge most, if not all, of the students would be coming for the first time. As every training college tutor knows, these youths must grapple with a great deal of new information in a comparatively short span of time; and some of this information is inevitably presented in capsule form. It will form a springboard for deeper excursions into particular periods and aspects of the history.

It is becoming more and more necessary for teacher educators (and other teachers at the tertiary level of education, to say nothing of the rest) to *write*, in the interest not only of their pupils but also of adults who have to depend on their own reading in the pursuit of further education.

It is noteworthy that the range and scope of literature on Jamaican education is growing, if slowly. Much of it is to be found in unpublished theses and dissertations produced in the University of the West Indies School of Education (and stored in the Documentation Centre). Mrs Whyte has herself produced one of these theses.

I wish the author the best of luck in this and future endeavours.

R. N. Murray,
Dean and Professor of Education,
University of the West Indies.

Contents

Preface   vii

Introduction   ix

I
The Slave Society   1

II
Emancipation—educational provision and the
    Negro Education Grant   7

III
Elementary education from the termination of the
    Negro Education Grant to 1962   14

IV
The growth of secondary education   31

V
Teacher education   42

VI
Attempts at higher education in Jamaica   55

VII
Technical, vocational and agricultural education   63

VIII
The management and control of education   76

IX
Development of teachers' organizations   94

X
Post-independence education   105

XI
The 'Education Thrust of the   115
Seventies' and after

Bibliography   161

Index   163

Preface

THE variety of views on what a book on the history of education should include makes it difficult for any one work to cover all aspects of this subject in a country. When the history of education was first introduced into the curriculum of teachers' training colleges, it was concerned chiefly with the history of educational ideas, and their influences on the education system of a country. In more recent times, the study of curriculum changes, textbooks, pupils' workbooks, school buildings, equipment and furniture has been considered as making a greater contribution to the understanding of our educational problems than the study of educational ideas. There is the view, too, that the history of education should deal with the influences of government policy on educational development and it is this aspect that will be emphasized in the following pages. Although education in Jamaica has passed through some very exciting periods, very little has been written about this aspect of the country's development. It was the difficulty of obtaining materials for a course in the history of education in Jamaica that forced me to prepare this manuscript. The work looks at landmarks in educational development in Jamaica since the seventeenth century, and lays the foundation for a more in depth study of the history of education in Jamaica. Studying a country's history helps its peoples to review their achievements and their failures. By so doing they should avoid the repetition of past mistakes. In the same way, a study of the history of educational development will help a country to measure its educational achievements and even re-examine suggestions for improvement that were ignored in former years.

M.I.W.

Introduction

THE history of a country's educational development must be seen in the context of its general history, since the establishment of educational institutions is influenced by religious, social, political and economic factors. Jamaica retains no trace of Spanish educational influence. Therefore the history of education in Jamaica will have to be accepted as commencing with the English period. During this period the society was stratified according to colour which determined social, economic and political status. The white minority population stood at the top of the social hierarchy while negro slaves who formed the majority of the population stood at the bottom. As formal education was not considered necessary for slaves, the first schools were set up for the white children. It was only when an attempt was made to spread the Christian religion among West Indian slaves that missionaries established schools for the teaching of the scriptures and reading. The missionaries met with much opposition from planters in their work. But the schools that they established during slavery made them gain recognition from the British government. Slavery was abolished in 1834. A year later, the missionaries were chosen to administer the Negro Education Grant which Parliament voted for the education of the newly emancipated slaves.

The grant marked the first attempt at government level to provide elementary education for the masses. It also established partnership between the government and the church in the provision of elementary and teacher education. During a period of economic strain in both Britain and the West Indies the grant was terminated. Subsequently, education in Jamaica had to depend on the churches until 1866 when there was a change from Assembly to Crown Colony Government. The new Government stimulated not only elementary and teacher education but all levels of education. Provisions were made to improve the efficiency of elementary schools and a boost was given to the teaching of agriculture throughout the period.

It was during this period that the first attempt was made to reorganize and control secondary education. Government appointed a permanent commission, the Jamaica Schools Commission, to manage endowments and see that they were beneficially administered. Institutions of Higher Education were operated for two different periods during the Crown Colony era.

It was this period, too, that saw a great number of enquiries into the education system at all levels. There were many recommendations but few were heeded. Since education was low in government priorities, its development was thwarted through lack of finance.

The economic depression of the early 1930s caused great hardship in the West Indies. Poor social and economic conditions among the labouring class led to much discontent. Attempts to organize labour resulted in riots throughout the British West Indies between 1935 and 1938.

The British government was alerted by the riots and so a Commission of Inquiry under Lord Moyne was appointed to investigate social and economic conditions and make recommendations. Great inadequacies in social and economic services were revealed in the report.

To improve the conditions the West Indian Welfare Fund was created. Under the scheme, an annual grant of £1,000,000 was made to the West Indies over a twenty-year period for the improvement of education, housing and communication. Much of this fund was spent on the improvement of facilities and curricula in schools but conditions remained unsatisfactory.

Educated members of the middle class became more and more disenchanted with Crown Colony Government. Their criticisms and demands helped to gain Representative Government for Jamaica in 1944. The New Constitution provided for greater participation in the government by the people. Therefore, the role of education in national development became greater than under the previous constitutions. The fact that the output of the education system would influence all other spheres of the government's activities had become evident.

Constitutional changes together with Welfare Funds gave impetus to all levels of education. The 1940s saw the extension of government aid to secondary schools and the establishment of a University College of the West Indies in Jamaica.

An increase in national income through the development of tourism, bauxite and other resources since the 1950s has made more funds available for education. But it was the achievement of independence in 1962 that intensified the move towards an educated society. The expansion of educational facilities was seen as the only way to meet the requirement for trained personnel at all levels.

A new era dawned for education in 1966 when the government proposed a 'New Deal for Education'. Changes in the lending policy of the World Bank caused Jamaica to obtain loans for the extension of educational facilities. Under the New Deal programme much consideration was given to the development of human resources as a major factor in the growth of the economy. With this in view, the expansion of secondary and post-secondary education became of utmost importance. Following the change of government in 1972, the New Deal was incorporated and extended into the Thrust for the Seventies. The latter plan has brought revolutionary changes to all levels of the education system.

I

The Slave Society

JAMAICA became known to Europeans in 1494 when the island was visited by a Spanish expedition under Christopher Columbus. At that time the inhabitants were a pre-literate people called Arawaks. The Spaniards were from a technologically more advanced society. Therefore the result of their impact on the Arawaks was not assimilation but destruction of the Arawaks and their culture.

It would seem that the policy of Spanish imperialism was to create replicas of Spanish towns in the colonies for the benefit of their colonists, and at the same time christianize the natives. The sovereigns of Spain had mentioned the latter in the offical aims of Columbus' second voyage. With this objective in view, monasteries and churches were established as centres of religious instruction.

The Spaniards were Roman Catholics so their religious influence disappeared with the arrival in 1655 of the English who were Protestants. Neither the Spaniards nor their slaves had the opportunity to intermingle with the English. Shortly after the arrival of the English, the Spaniards were driven from Jamaica, and their slaves found shelter in the mountains. The English did however perpetuate the slave society started by the Spaniards.

Offers of free land, mining rights, and retention of British citizenship attracted English colonists to Jamaica during the seventeenth and eighteenth centuries. Their number was increased by white indentured servants who came for contractual employment, but later became permanent residents. The expansion of the sugar industry attracted more and more people to Jamaica, including an increasing number of African slaves.

The population became class and colour structured. At the top of the hierarchy was the white minority population. Among them were the governor and his councillors, civil servants, planters, estate employees and soldiers. They represented political, economic and social power. The majority of the population were slaves and they stood at the bottom of the class structure. So low was their status that they were counted with the stock of the estates. Not many female white immigrants entered the West Indies during slavery. As a result, the white male found companionship with the slave women. From this interbreeding of negroes and whites came the coloured population. Although for a time they were deprived of many of the privileges of the white population, their fathers freed some of them from the shackles of slavery. Many of them acquired wealth and education and emerged as the middle class of Jamaican society. By the middle of the eighteenth century, the whites were fearing both their numerical and their economic strength.

It was evident that educational provision in pre-emancipation Jamaica would be considered for the top and middle classes. Members of the top class would have wanted some form of education for both their white and their coloured children since they hailed from a society where this was the custom of their group.

A glance at some of the accounts of the slavery period in Jamaica shows that although benefactions were made for education, the authorities were rather slow in using them for such purposes. Bridges, the historian (1717), reported that charitable donations in the island amounted to over £9,000 plus lands and dwellings. Among the earliest bequests was one of £100 made by Sir Henry Morgan in 1688. It was intended to supplement £100 given by one Joachin Hane to establish a school in the parish of St Mary. Apparently, these donations remained unused. In 1740, Leslie, another historian, observed that there was no 'Public School' in the whole island. The benefactor to one school in the parish of St John was one Colonel Coape, a member of the Legislative Council. He provided £100 per annum as payment to the schoolmaster, Mr Lemon.

The coming of English rule to Jamaica meant that the Anglican faith would replace that of the Roman Catholics. Anglican ministers from England were given cures in Jamaica and were paid their stipends from the island's treasury. Gardner stated that some of these clergymen kept schools to supplement their stipends. Following the custom in England, they were required to get a licence from the Bishop of the Anglican Church to permit them to teach. The Bishop had power to examine their learning, morality, and religious fervour, but this rule was not enforced.

When the Protestant missionaries came to Jamaica, they too started to keep school. These schools were described as seldom of a high order, and little better than the Dame Schools in England. The latter were kept by elderly women, and their most important role was child-minding. An exceptional school of the period was the Metropolitan in Spanish Town founded in 1825 by James Phillippo, a Baptist missionary. Latrobe, A British Inspector of Schools who visited Jamaica in 1838, described it as a superior type school.

These early schools were patronized by those whites who could not afford to send their children to England for an education, but the practice proved expensive. Not everyone was in favour of obtaining education in this way. As Long, an eighteenth century historian, noted, the education that children received in England did not prepare them for any useful occupation unless they followed the professions. He said that many of them 'learned to renounce their native place, their parents, and their friends'. As was the custom in England, a few Jamaican families had governesses to teach their girls music, writing and the feminine graces. The local schools could not have been of a high standard as the office of a teacher was viewed with contempt.

Many of the older Grammar Schools had their genesis in the bequests of the seventeenth and eighteenth centuries. The mismanagement and neglect of these bequests must have come to the attention of the government. In 1791, a Committee of the Legislative Council was set up to inquire into them. Owing to the Council's lack of interest in education, a report was submitted only for St Ann where in 1721 Charles Drax had bequeathed his estate to establish a Free School for eight poor boys and eight poor girls. Nothing more was heard of these bequests until 1825 when several of them were submitted to the Assembly. Those in favour of Wolmers School included the estates of William Crosse and J. O. Luskie as well as sums varying from £100 to £1,000. Robert Munro left his residuary estate for two school in St Elizabeth. Other donations were for Mannings Free School, and a School for the poor at

Vere. These schools were to be established for the benefit of free people.

No consideration was given by anyone in society to schools for slave children during the greater part of the pre-emancipation period. Only informal education was available for them. Groups of very young children were minded by aged slave women until they were old enough to join the work-gangs on the estates.

It was the idea that all men are equal which stimulated the movement against negro slavery. Out of this idea came also the Missionary Societies—the Baptist in 1792, the London Missionary Society in 1795, and the British and Foreign Bible Society in 1802. These were the societies that sent missionaries to the West Indies with a view to christianizing the heathen slaves.

During the eighteenth century, Sunday Schools were started in England for children who worked in factories and had Sunday as their free day. In addition to Reading and Catechism, some of them were taught Arithmetic and Writing. Missionaries in Jamaica followed this pattern and used the Sunday School as the earliest source of education for slave children. Evening and Day Schools followed Sunday Schools where these were possbile. But the missionaries faced opposition from the planters. It was felt by the latter that instruction would make the slave aware of his human worth, and prevent him from being a 'good slave'. Some children got a mere three or four hours tuition each week. Such a short period could barely arouse their desire for learning.

In his assessment of educational provision in the West Indies in 1834, Rev. John Sterling described the school situation as one with poor buildings, large classes, poor and untrained teachers, and senseless methods of rote learning. He was doubtful of the competence of teachers as many of them turned to teaching after they had failed in every other occupation. In the case of the Methodists, teachers were drawn from able class leaders. With the absence of teacher training facilities and adequate educational background the competence of these teachers could not have been far removed from that of their pupils.

The missionary schools placed much emphasis on learning the Catechism and reading selected verses from the Bible. There no doubt that this initial curriculum instilled a religious flavour in the education system.

II

Emancipation—
educational provision and the
Negro Education Grant

In August 1833 an Act for the Abolition of Slavery in the British colonies was passed by the British Parliament. Among its clauses was one providing for the moral and religious education of the negro population upon liberal and comprehensive principles. Two years later, a grant of £30,000 annually was made to the colonies for negro education. It was called the Negro Education Grant. After 1840 the grant was gradually decreased and was withdrawn in 1845.

The size of the grant allotted to a territory was based on the number of its ex-slaves. Jamaica received £7,500 in 1835. At first the British government was undecided as to who should administer the grant. The choice lay between the Assembly and the missionaries. While the Assembly had no machinery for such a job, the missionaries were already involved in educational work in the colonies. With the aid of funds from their headquarters in England they had been establishing schools where conditions proved favourable.

Rev. John Sterling who had worked in St Kitts was asked by the British government to assess educational provision in the British West Indies. This he did from returns sent to him by the religious denominations. In his assessment, he regarded the churches as great promoters of education among the young who had been neglected. He felt that the teaching ability of the missionary teachers was of a low standard. He saw the readiness to undertake the teaching job as their main qualification. On the other hand, he felt that Assemblies that were comprised of planters would not support the education of slaves when they needed them to work on the estates. Furthermore, there was no public department concerned with education. Bearing all these factors in mind, he recommended that the funds for education be given to the churches.

Rev. John Sterling foresaw disadvantages accruing to education if government were to handle the project. For one thing, the voluntary agencies were likely to withdraw their contributions. Besides, education would lose the religious base given by the various religious denominations.

Suggestions to ensure the efficiency of the system were also submitted by Rev. Sterling. If schools were to be efficient, he suggested that government aid be withheld when a denomination wanted to set up schools in areas that were well supplied with them. Each denomination had a tendency to establish schools for its adherents. As a result several small inefficient schools could be found in a small district. This was at a time when schools charged fees. Rev. Sterling suggested that this be introduced gradually so as not to discourage school attendance. The only compulsory payment suggested was that for writing as this skill was considered by the authorities to be of little value to the poor.

As a further means of securing efficiency, he suggested the institution of frequent inspections. Areas of inspection were to include the moral conduct of a teacher, the number of pupils, their regularity of attendance and the curriculum. He also recommended that attendance be made the determinant of the size of grants to schools. It is worth noting that the use of attendance as the basis for grants to schools continued into the twentieth century.

Although the British government had made the grant primarily for the education of the masses, Rev. Sterling saw the need for higher grade schools which would complete the work of the primary schools. These schools should be for the age-group ten to eighteen years, fee-paying and available to all classes. Government grants should be given to make these schools subject to inspection. The curriculum should include the three R's, Book-keeping, English History and Geography, with rudiments of Natural History, Natural Philosophy and Mathematics. No consideration was given to this aspect of Sterling's suggestion.

Realising that any plan for education would be impracticable without a corps of native teachers, Rev. Sterling suggested the establishment of a Normal School in Jamaica. The principal should be a religious person, though not necessarily a minister of religion. Students were to be recommended by the denominations. But an entrance examination was considered necessary. Government's responsibility was seen as that of aiding students financially and meeting the cost of salaries.

Administration and problems of the Negro Education Grant

The first allocation of the Negro Education Grant was in respect of buildings. In addition to being used as Day Schools, they could be used for Infant, Noon and Adult

Classes as well as Sunday Schools. The fact that children and adults alike attended school, accounted for these periods of schooling.

As recommended by Rev. Sterling, the missionary societies of the various denominations were chosen to administer the grant. Among them were the Society for the Propagation of the Gospel, the London Missionary Society, the Church Missionary Society and the Methodist Society. The Mico Charity which provided Normal Schools as well as Elementary Schools also qualified for grants. A society was given two-thirds the cost of each school building constructed under the programme. It was expected that these schools would devote their time to Reading, Writing and Arithmetic, and Catechetical and other instruction in the Principles of Religion. But there were schools that included Geography, Grammar and Needle-work in their curriculum. For instance the Metropolitan School taught Scripture, History, General Knowledge and General Science.

Bearing in mind the need for efficiency, inspectors were appointed to supervise the schools. This was done on a denominational basis. Schools sponsored by the Society for the Propagation of the Gospel were inspected by the magistrates and the Bishop and clergy of the Anglican Church. The Church Missionary Society and the Mico Charity appointed their own inspectors.

Teachers employed in the schools were of several categories. There were Europeans sent out by the parent missionary societies in England. Other white persons resident in the island also did some teaching. Then there were the adult coloured persons who were sufficiently literate to conduct schools, and the young people who received training at the Normal Schools or larger Elementary Schools. The Metropolitan was one of the Elementary Schools that had a teacher-training department. The standard of these teachers was somewhat low. It is said that many of them had no other qualification than the willingness to teach. But so great was the need for teachers that there was no difficulty in entering the profession.

Conscious of the need for local teachers, the promoters of the Negro Education Grant made £5,000 available for teacher training. It was at this time, too, that the Lady Mico Charity established Normal Schools in Jamaica. There was much rivalry and division among the denominations in their search for adherents, so each established its own Normal School to train its teachers. The denominations as well as the Mico Charity received aid from the Negro Education Grant for this venture. The curriculum of the early Normal Schools had to be adapted to the educational level of the students. Many of them would have been barely literate after their brief exposure to education. As the emphasis was on moral and religious education, the Bible was the main textbook. Students were taught to read the Bible, sing hymns, memorize catechisms, and get a knowledge of Biblical Geography. Practical Teaching was also confined to Bible Lessons.

In the first instance, the Negro Education Grant was made available solely for school buildings. Therefore, the denominations had to meet recurrent expenses including teachers' salaries from their own resources. Faced with the problem of meeting expenses, the denominations were to learn that buildings alone cannot provide an education system. They therefore asked the authorities to make a part of the grant available for teachers' salaries. This request was granted. Consequently, the denominations were relieved of one-third of the cost of teachers' salaries.

In 1838, the British Government sent out Latrobe, an Inspector of Schools, to assess the working of the education system. He found many obstacles in the path of progress. For one thing, he was disappointed at the small number of school buildings that had been completed. In many cases the cost of buildings had been underestimated. There were also problems of getting labour and titles to land. Furthermore, rivalry amongst the denominations resulted in a waste of resources as two or more denominations sometimes sited schools in thinly populated districts. At the same time, the denominations were so self-centred that they remained ignorant of one another's activities. When the denominations started their building programme, they found it convenient to build schools near the estates or on the coast. The newly freed slaves tended to move away from the estates and establish themselves in the hills. This migration put the schools out of their reach.

Another problem of the period was that of irregular attendance. Pupils attended school regularly from Tuesday to Thursday. On Monday, they remained at home to help their parents. The introduction of compulsory education recommended by Rev. Sterling did not pass beyond the stage of consideration by the legislature.

Latrobe was disturbed at the poor quality of teachers and the inadequate provision made for their maintenance. As Rev. Knight pointed out in *Liberty and Progress*, many Normal School students, though as old as their tutors, were illiterate. With the low level of entry, it was difficult to produce good teachers in the short time devoted to their training. It was unlikely too, that the local teaching force would attract suitable recruits when their European counterparts were paid twice their salaries. A European teacher's salary was about two hundred pounds per annum. It was the high cost of securing teachers from England that prompted the missionaries to establish local Normal Schools.

Another difficulty that Latrobe found in the path of popular education was the fact that some planters in Jamaican society were still prejudiced against the labouring class getting an education. He claimed that they showed this by doing nothing to help the cause of negro education.

Latrobe praised the Baptists who as a group rejected aid and still provided education for their adherents. He felt that the other missionary societies were also capable of this performance.

A blow struck missionary efforts in 1841 when the withdrawal of the Negro Education Grant was announced. This meant that the responsibility for financing education had to be placed on the churches and legislature. The Grant had certainly helped to establish the idea of popular education in the British West Indies. Once this had been done, someone had to keep it alive. The years ahead were to show that the responsibility for education continued to be shared between the government and the churches. The churches continued to maintain their schools, despite financial hardships in both England and the colonies. The Jamaican Assembly showed awareness of its responsibility by establishing an Education Board in 1843 and voting one thousand pounds for educational purposes.

III
Elementary education from the termination of the Negro Education Grant to 1962

Elementary education 1845–1866

IN 1845 when the Negro Education Grant was discontinued, the British West Indies were still lacking in the basic social services. The transition from estate responsibility to government responsibility was long and slow. The awareness of the importance of education had barely begun to emerge in a society where education had to compete with other social services for very limited financial resources.

Both the Colonial Office and the Jamaica Assembly advocated an education system with emphasis on industrial education for the newly freed people. Industrial instruction at that time was equivalent to agricultural training. As a means of encouraging the teaching of agriculture a grant of thirty pounds was made to schools that taught agriculture to more than fifty pupils for at least a year.

The prevalence of destitute and vagrant children gave much concern to the government. Industrial schools were therefore established to care for them. The introduction of industrial instruction in schools did not meet with much success. Reporting in 1847 the inspector of schools was alarmed at its failure. This he attributed to such factors as the lack of an artificial supply of water, the distance children had to walk to school, and the need for them to assist their parents in cultivating their plots at week-ends.

During this period the denominations continued to maintain their schools. In addition to the denominational schools there were Vestry Schools maintained by grants from the Vestry—the local government body of the time.

One admirable feature of the period was the expression of self-help. Groups of parents built schools and formed their own committees for employing teachers and running the school.

The period 1845–65 was one of great economic strain for Jamaica. Like the rest of the British colonies she lost preferential treatment for sugar in the British market. This led to a reduction in the financial returns from sugar which was the mainstay of the economy. The island's revenue was also affected, and a declining revenue meant very little funds for education. The economy was further weakened by droughts and epidemics of cholera and smallpox. Along with these problems went increasing unemployment and low wages. With poverty among the peasants, schools were hit by irregular and poor attendance. The denominations too, found themselves with little funds. These conditions certainly placed education in the doldrums during this period.

Reforms under Crown Colony Government

The Morant Bay Rebellion was a people's reaction to the distressing experiences that they had gone through since emancipation. On the one hand, it marked the end of an era of political, social and economic dominance by the white population. On the other, it began an era when the

Metropolitan Government and its local representatives were made to realize that the peasants had needs as well as the ability to express them. The representative system of government which had existed in the island for over two centuries, was replaced by a Crown Colony Government. This change put an end to the frequent divisions between the Assembly and the Council and set the stage for reforms which were to transform several conditions in the island. Under the able governor, Sir John Peter Grant, several reforms were made in the field of education.

During the period of representative government, the Anglican Church was maintained by government. One of the first steps taken by the Crown Colony administration was the disestablishment of the Anglican Church. The funds were transferred to educational purposes. This move met with the approval of the other demominations who felt that the Anglican Schools were accorded financial advantages from which they were barred.

Another concern of the Crown Colony administration was the low standard of efficiency in education. The Payment by Results system was therefore introduced in 1867 to upgrade the efficiency of Elementary Schools. Grants earned by schools were made dependent on the quality of the pupils' work as well as the size and regularity of school attendance. Under the system, pupils of a school were examined for one day to determine the school's classification. An inspector would examine six or seven classes in eight subjects and then award marks according to the quality and quantity of work done by the pupils. A school gained a maximum of eighty-four marks. They were divided among the following subjects:

Subjects	Marks	
Chief subjects		
Reading	12	
Writing from Dictation	12	36 marks
Arithmetic	12	
Secondary subjects		
Writing	6	
Scripture Knowledge	6	
General Knowledge	6	
Grammar	6	48 marks
Geography	6	
Singing	6	
Organization	6	
Discipline	6	

It was expected that teachers would spend more time on the chief subjects than on the secondary ones. Schools were graded on the basis of marks as follows:

Marks	Grades
56 and over	first class
44–55	second class
32–43	third class
Below 32	not classified

Under the 1867 Regulations, a school could obtain two sets of grants. One grant was based on average attendance, while the other was based on the quality of the work done in the school. These were the grants:

Type of school	Average attendance	Quality of work
First class	6s. per unit	£20 per school
Second class	5s. per unit	£15 per school
Third class	4s. per unit	£10 per school

By 1916 teachers' salaries were paid from a number of grants that the Education Department awarded to schools. These were based on marks and average attendance. A Merit Grant was awarded for marks obtained at the annual one-day inspection. It was calculated according to the following scale:

Annual average attendance	Grant per mark
Below 60	15s.
Above 60	20s.

This grant formed the major part of the principal teacher's salary. Average attendance formed the sole basis of the salary for assistant teachers. These were the rates per unit of average attendance:

Annual average attendance	Grant per unit of average attendance
51–70	6s.
over 70	12s.
over 250	4s. per average attendance above 80

Schools with average attendance above 60 were paid an additional three shillings per unit of average attendance above that number. This grant was used for the salaries of both principal and assistant teachers.

Additional grants were given to teachers who were holders of certificates. They were paid a higher grant than uncertificated teachers for marks above 49.

Type of certificate	Date of award	Marks	Payment per mark
First class or good service	Prior to March 1918	49	20s.
First class		Above 55	25s.
Second class Good service in second class schools	After 1901	Above 49	12s. 6d.

The above grants were paid to certificated principal teachers who had been in charge of the schools earning the grants for at least six months. Certificated assistant teachers were paid half the grant paid to principal teachers. Certificates were awarded to teachers who passed training college examinations and gave satisfactory service over a number of years. The Good Service Certificate was awarded to a teacher who gave satisfactory service over a period of twelve years without passing any training college examinations.

Extra grants were earned by schools which included Sewing, Manual Training and Gardening in their curriculum. Schools that taught Sewing earned three shillings for each girl in average attendance. This grant was used for the payment of teachers who taught this subject.

In the case of Gardening, one penny could be earned for each boy in average attendance plus an initial grant of forty five shillings for tools, and an annual grant of six pounds.

The grants for Manual Training were higher than those for Gardening and Sewing. There was an initial grant of thirty pounds plus a grant of fifteen pounds for an average attendance at the Manual Training Class of between 15 and 19 pupils, and twenty pounds when the average attendance reached twenty. Five shillings per unit of average attendance was also obtainable for the maintenance of tools.

Average attendance was the basis on which schools were staffed. This was the teacher-pupil ratio up to 1918:

Grade	Number of pupils
Head Teacher	70
Registered Principal	70
Registered Assistant I	60
Registered Assistant II	40
Unregistered Assistant	30
Pupil Teacher	20

The Payment by Results System was unsatisfactory in its achievement. The first recommendation for its abolition was made by the Lumb Commission in 1898. After that date several attempts were made by the Jamaica Union of Teachers to get it abolished. This was done in 1920 when a system of fixed salaries and graded schools and teachers was introduced. Under the new system teachers' salaries began to be determined by their qualifications, efficiency and length of service while schools were graded on the basis of average attendance.

Opening grants

A census taken in 1867 showed that there were 236 grant-aided schools, and 158 schools that received no aid. In 1870, the institution of opening grants caused a steady increase in the number of schools. These opening grants were specially made for the erection of schools. The scheme proved successful, as by 1885 the number of grant-aided schools had more than doubled.

Model schools

Model schools were established to provide increased training facilities for teachers. These were normally practising schools attached to training colleges. But between 1870 and 1876, they were used by the government as models for Elementary School teachers. They were intended to supplement provisions for Elementary Schools as well as demonstrate efficient school managment for the guidance and instruction of teachers in the surrounding districts. At the same time, they were used to train young teachers. Model schools established during the period were Port Maria, Bath, Falmouth, Montego Bay, Charles Town and Port Antonio. The model masters were recruited from

England, and like other Elementary School teachers, they earned their grants through Payment by Results.

A further boost was given to industrial education during the Crown Colony period. Sir John Peter Grant was directed by the Secretary of State for the Colonies to explore the possibility of combining industrial training with elementary education. Under Payment by Results, schools that devoted a minimum of three hours daily to manual labour were classified as Industrial Schools. The pupils were relieved of paying fees and the school's grant was fifty per cent more than that of similarly graded Elementary Schools. Between 1867 and 1872 the number of Industrial Schools was doubled. After that time there was a reduction in their grants because schools failed to give satisfactory results. This was attributed to the teachers' lack of knowledge in Agriculture.

There was much controversy as to the importance of agriculture at that time. For one thing, the proprietors of the estates craved for an education system which would instil habits of industry in the population. At the same time missionaries and some local legislators felt that such an education would limit the upward mobility of the peasants.

The Crown Colony Period was extremely fertile for investigations of the education system. This could be considered as a necessary precondition for reform. But the findings and recommendations were repeated throughout the period with very few implementations. Lack of funds was the reason given for ignoring the changes recommended. Most of the investigations took the form of interviews with people in education and relevant fields.

A report on the condition of the juvenile population in Jamaica in 1879 revealed the incidence of extensive vagrancy. Lack of parental control, unstable families and poverty were blamed for this condition. The institution of compulsory education, district school boards, a conscience clause, government schools and the increase in industrial schools, were among its recommendations. The establishment of a government college for women was also suggested. This last recommendation was implemented in 1885 when Shortwood College was established.

A Royal Commission in 1883 was not satisfied with the outcome of increasing expenditure on education. It was found that increasing expenditure on education over the period 1862–1881 was not commensurate with the degree of literacy achieved. While expenditure on education had been increased six times, the number of illiterates had doubled.

The next major report was that of Lumb in 1898. As chairman of the Commission, Judge Lumb carried out a thorough examination of the Jamaican system of education after thirty years of the Payment by Results System. The Commission was to report on the suitability of the education system to the needs of the country, and to suggest ways in which both economy and efficiency could be maintained in the system.

In the report, the highest priority was given to the establishment of an efficient system of primary education. This was to be achieved by the amalgamation of the smaller and less efficient schools and the establishment of government schools in place of aid to new voluntary schools. Compulsory education was suggested with a view to preventing waste of funds through irregular attendance. This was to be extended over a six-year period, beginning with the six-year olds. A school age population of six to twelve years instead of five to fourteen years was suggested, to increase the number of children in that age group who would benefit from schooling. Of particular importance were suggestions for the reorganization of the curriculum.

The curriculum was thought to be extensive and the teaching superficial. It was recommended that more attention be paid to Reading, and that it be co-ordinated with other subjects. Physical Drill, Singing, and Drawing were to be introduced in the schools and Domestic Economy and Manual and Agricultural instruction were to be made an integral part of the curriculum. Most of the recommendations for securing efficiency in primary education were not implemented before the next inquiry. A lame attempt at compulsory education was made in 1912 when it was introduced in a few population centres. The non-observers of the law were seldom penalized, and so far the problem of irregular attendance continued unchecked. The amalgamation of schools took place, and the number fell from 962 in 1895 to 653 in 1934.

The importance of education in the over-all development of any country cannot be over-estimated. Major Wood, Under Secretary of State, who visited the island in 1922 to assess the strength of the country's demand for a representative government, registered his criticism of the education system. He found that the Elementary School curriculum tended to be too elaborate and that 'as regards curriculum and textbooks, dependence upon English publication is the rule.' As far as the Jamaican situation was concerned, he recommended the preparation of reading material in Local History, Geography, Hygiene and Gardening and the addition of Sanitation and Hygiene to the curriculum.

Criticism of elementary education was aired more frequently than that of other levels. This is understandable since the majority of the population did not go beyond the elementary level. Dissatisfaction reached its height in 1926 when suggestions for an investigation of the system came from three sources.

The Hon. P. W. Sangster, Member of the Legislative Council for Hanover, summoned managers and teachers in that parish to a meeting to discuss possible causes of dissatisfaction. He proposed to examine whether or not the curriculum was overcrowded, and if so, which subjects should be eliminated, whether or not Science should include Agriculture and Personal Hygiene, and the advisability of establishing Central, Industrial and Continuation County Schools. A resolution was moved in the 1926 Jamaica Union of Teachers' Conference for the appointment of a Committee to inquire into the causes of dissatisfaction with elementary education.

Being aware of the criticisms directed at education the Hon. J. T. Cawley introduced a motion in the Legislative Council for the appointment of a Select Committee on Education. The motion stated:

That in view of the expressed dissatisfaction with the existing system of Elementary Education in Jamaica, and the apparent need of a more practical curriculum which would embody Technical and Continuation Schools thereby fitting boys and girls of the Colony whose only avenue of education is the Elementary School, to their proper place as citizens and to enable them to earn a competent living.

Be it resolved that a Select Committee of this Council be appointed to deal with the matter and report as soon as possible.

The Committee arrived at its findings through reports,

evidence from witnesses and visits to schools. Witnesses were drawn from the Education Department, the Board of Education, Schools and Managers of Schools Boards. Despite Lumb's recommendations, there was still no provision for Games, and Practical Agriculture. The latter ceased to be a special subject with the abolition of Payment by Results and so was neglected. The Committee suggested that Agricultural Instructors should assist in the teaching of Agriculture and that the curriculum should be adapted to the needs of the environment. The absence of reference to Jamaicans who had been leaders in the country were criticized.

The recommendations were not implemented and were repeated four years later by Hammond, Director of Education. Hammond gave a most depressing picture of the standard of elementary education. He described the system as aimless and foreign to the people it was intended to serve. His view was that the absence of provision for curriculum studies and the writing of textbooks retarded the development of education. He saw the curriculum as 'bookish' with but few books and unrelated to the present experiences and future needs of the island's children. Following Lumb's suggestion, he recommended that the school-leaving age be reduced from fourteen to twelve years, and that the curriculum be simplified. This would enable teachers to cope with large classes and reduce the problem of illiteracy. Localized schools with provision for teaching Agriculture and Domestic Economy were to be established to cater for children in the age-group of twelve to fifteen years. These schools would provide post-primary training for the majority of the island's children as secondary education was available for a very small percentage of them.

The 1930s were years of economic depression for the entire world. Very little improvement was made in elementary education. Although Hammond's report reached the legislature, his recommendations were not implemented. Experience of poverty, low wages and unemployment sparked off a series of riots and disturbances in the West Indies.

As a result, a Royal Commission under Lord Moyne was appointed to investigate social and economic conditions and make recommendations. The commission was specifically asked to present a memorandum on elementary education in Jamaica. This was to include a survey of accomplishments in the past hundred years, difficulties resulting from social and economic conditions, and the policy pursued for widening the scope of educational services in order to make the school the centre of communal life and progress in conjunction with other agencies of the community. The Commission blamed the difficulty of formulating policy on the dividing of responsibility for education between government and the denominations.

The curriculum of the schools was still found to be unrelated to the needs of society. Too much stress was said to be placed on literary work with the consequent neglect of practical work.

In its recommendations, the Commission suggested the simplification and revision of the curriculum with more reference to the West Indies. History and Geography were to include a knowledge of local topography and historical monuments. In the later stage of primary school, practical and agricultural subjects were to be introduced.

The Commission was concerned about the health of the island's children. As a means of improving their condition, it was suggested that physical training be linked with the provision of playgrounds and food for the under-nourished. In addition, hygiene and health education were to be considered both theoretically and practically. As a means of ensuring the latter, school meals were to be provided for children.

In the matter of school organization it was recommended that schools be graded as Primary and Junior Secondary, and that Supervisory Officers be attached to the Department of Education. Primary Schools should provide for the age-group six to twelve years and Junior Secondary Schools for the age-group twelve to fifteen years. It was further suggested that play-centres and Nursery Schools be attached to Primary Schools. These centres were to be staffed by qualified Kindergarten Mistresses assisted by older girls who were to be taught child welfare. There were recommendations too for improvement in school buildings, water supply, sanitation and provision of equipment.

Elementary education under Representative Government 1944–1962

In 1944, a new constitution was granted to Jamaica. Crown Colony Government was replaced by Representative Government. Instead of a semi-representative one-chambered legislature there were two chambers, one elected and one nominated. For the first time in the history of Jamaica all adults of twenty-one years and over were given the franchise. The constitution provided for an Executive Council of five nominated members and five elected members. The five elected members were referred to as Ministers, and among them was a Minister of Education (Hon. J. A. McPherson). This type of constitution provided for greater representation of the people's interest. At the same time, there was the necessity for an enfranchized population to be literate. For this to be achieved, the authorities realized that greater emphasis would have to be placed on education.

The problem of finance had always stifled the development of education in Jamaica. As a result of the Moyne Commission report published in 1945 a Colonial Development and Welfare Fund was established to finance social and economic development in the West Indies. These funds stimulated educational development.

The 1944 hurricane destroyed many school buildings. At the Jubilee Dinner of the Jamaica Union of Teachers that year, the Governor announced that the United Kingdom Government had voted £500,000 for the reconstruction of school buildings. Since the condition of Elementary School buildings had always drawn harsh criticisms from all who reported on education, it is evident that such news was received with jubilation.

The need for the expansion of infant education and the reorganization of the Elementary School curriculum to make it more relevant to the needs of society was stressed by everyone who commented on the education system. The 1939 Hansard Reports recommended an increase in the number of Infant Schools or a lowering of the entrance age to Elementary Schools. Attempts were made to meet these needs during the period of Representative Government. In 1944, funds were made available for the establishment of Infant Centres where local support could supplement small government grants. The Child Welfare Association also agreed to sponsor Infant Centres. It was felt that the basis for agricultural training could be laid in the Lower Division of Elementary School by including Nature Study in the curriculum. Efforts to introduce

Agriculture in the later years of Elementary School life had not been successful.

The introduction of practical subjects in the school curriculum was given much priority at this time. These included Domestic Science, Agriculture and Manual Training. The rapid changes which took place regarding the emphasis on practical subjects are indicated in the increased numbers below:

Centres and projects	1944	1955
Manual Training	15	125
Domestic Science	1	239
Art and Crafts	–	4

Physical Education, too, was given recognition, and funds were made available for equipment for sports and games.

The necessity for children to acquire a knowledge of their political rights and privileges made a claim for the inclusion of Civics in the curriculum for the Upper Division of the Elementary School. As a result, a Manual for Civics was compiled.

Some attention was paid to the nutritional state of school children. For a long time unsuccessful petitions were made to government to provide school meals for destitute children. At last, school meals were subsidized by government and kitchens attached to many schools. Hot mid-day meals were provided, and so the kitchens were initially called soup kitchens. These were the fore-runners of our present school canteens.

It was during this period that Senior Schools were established to separate children over twelve years from those under twelve years. They provided more specific and practical education for thousands of children who were unable to find places in Secondary Schools. At the same time most children in Secondary Schools had to pay fees while education in the Senior Schools was free. It was unfortunate that these schools were sited only in urban areas, so their beneficial influence was limited. It is noteworthy, too, that two Senior Schools—Kingston and May Pen—were selected to carry out an experiment in secondary education. They successfully prepared students for the Cambridge Local Examinations.

Prior to 1944, provision for education seemed to have been of a residual nature. Departments such as Prisons and Public Works were provided for more adequately. It is significant that a national awareness of the importance of education started to emerge in 1944. This was shown in the major role that education obtained in the formulation of National Plans produced by the Government after 1944.

IV

The growth
of secondary education

THE early benefactors of education in Jamaica were concerned with the education of free people. Most of the endowments were made for the benefit of the white population who lacked the financial means to obtain an education in England. Unfortunately, society was not sufficiently education-conscious to carry out the will of the benefactors, so many endowments were either mismanaged or not utilized at all. The existence of the following endowments was reported at the end of the eighteenth century:

Date	Benefactor	Original school	Surviving school
1694	Raines Waites	Alley and Manchester	
1744	P. Beckford	Beckford and Smith	St Jago
1830	Hon. Smith	Smith	
1736	John Wolmer	Wolmer's	Wolmer's
1770	Martin Rusea	Rusea Free	Rusea's
1785		Titchfield	Titchfield
1795	Charles Drax	Walton Free	Jamaica College
1730	Thomas Manning	Mannings	Mannings
1738	Sir Nicholas Lawes	School at Half-Way-Tree	

Date	Benefactor	Original school	Surviving school
1740		Vere and Manchester Free Schools	
1721	Charles Drax	Drax Free School	Jamaica College
1797	Munro	Rotsdam	Munro
1825	Dickenson	Malvern	Hampton

These schools were established to provide the white population with education similar to that available in England. The teachers were from England and the curriculum of the schools was copied from the English models.

While the Negro Education Grant assisted the churches in their provision of elementary and teacher education, no assistance was given to churches in their attempt to provide secondary education during the latter part of the nineteenth century. The increasing provision of Elementary School places resulting from the Payment by Results System meant that there was increased demand for secondary schools. In the churches' attempt to meet this demand, the following schools were established:

Date	Founder	School
1843	Baptist	Calabar
1850	Roman Catholic (Society of Jesus)	St Georges'
1858	Roman Catholic (Franciscan Sisters)	Immaculate Conception
1876	Methodist	York Castle
1875	Anglicans	St Hilda's
1897	Anglicans	Cathedral High
1882	Baptists	Westwood
1898	Religious Society of Friends	Happy Grove

Institutions such as York Castle and Calabar provided High School, Theological and Teacher Education.

The Crown Colony Government instituted reforms at all levels of education. But the previous government took over educational endowments in 1865. Annuities of between six and ten per cent on capital were paid to the trusts responsible for administering the schools. Further reorganization of the control of secondary schools took place in 1879 when the Jamaica Schools Commission was established. This was a corporate body appointed by the Governor and empowered to control endowments and establish schools according to the will of benefactors. Its first act was the taking over of the funds and property of the Jamaica Free School, formerly Drax Free School. It was empowered to make regulations governing the admittance and dismissal of scholars. The course of study, discipline and financing of school programmes were also placed under its control.

The Jamaica Free School was transferred to Kingston where it was renamed the Jamaica High School and became the first Secondary School to receive a grant under the Crown Colony administration. It was placed at the top of the hierarchy of secondary schools in the island. Its curriculum was upgraded, and new curricula were drawn up for other trust schools. A system of foundations was created. This enabled students from trust schools of a lower academic level to go to Jamaica High School.

Lower level schools were termed Middle Grade Schools. Among them were Beckford and Smith, Titchfield and Mannings. Following the upgrading of the Jamaica High School, other schools were reorganized and new Boards of Trustees appointed to manage them. Some Trust Funds were used to maintain Infant Schools,

Elementary Schools, Boys and Girls Secondary Departments as well as provide Scholarships to the Jamaica High School. For instance, the Titchfield and Vere Trust Funds were used for all these purposes. In addition to scholarships provided from the Trust Funds, six scholarships were offered by the government to students from Secondary and Elementary Schools and made tenable at the Jamaica High School.

Shortly after the establishment of the Jamaica School Commission, the Cambridge Local Examinations were introduced into the island. As this was an English-based and controlled examination, the English Grammar School curriculum had to slavishly followed. Textbooks compiled in English had to be used and a large proportion of the Jamaican Grammar School staff were teachers recruited from England. The use of this examination in Jamaica marked the beginning of years of imitation of English patterns and thought in education without any consideration of their relevance to the country's needs.

It is evident that in the eighteenth century schools were sited in parishes where benefactions were made. Schools established by the religious denominations were sited in populous areas. On this basis, many areas would have been without Secondary Schools. Under the Secondary Education Law of 1892 the government attempted to meet this need. Provision was made for the government to establish Secondary Schools in populous areas where none existed. It is surprising that for many years to come just one school was established under the law. This was Montego Bay Boy's School, now Cornwall College.

The recommendations of the Lumb Commission, which gave priority to Primary Schools and suggested that Secondary Schools be established when finances were available, could have influenced the government's attitude to the provision of Secondary Schools. Furthermore, the sugar industry was experiencing difficulties, and funds for any kind of development, particularly education, would have been difficult to raise.

It was the duty of the Colonial Office to keep itself informed about the condition of the colonies. This explains the number of inquiries that were made from time to time. In 1911, Piggott, an English Inspector of Schools, visited Jamaica to inspect Secondary Schools and make recommendations for their improvement. He commented on the wide variation in control that the Jamaica Schools Commission exercised over Secondary Schools. Some schools were managed by local boards, others by trustees, and some by the religious denominations. He recommended that schools be governed by common clauses and that the Director of Education be made a member of all bodies governing the schools.

The incidence of sex discrimination did not escape Inspector Piggott's notice. Although there were two girls' schools and three mixed schools controlled by the Jamaica Schools Commission, no woman representative was on the commission. In the area of scholarships for Higher Education, there were the Rhodes, Jamaica and two Sixty-Pound Scholarships. None of these was offered to girls. He suggested that one of the last named should be offered to a girl.

In the matter of curricula he found those followed by the schools too elaborate. Some schools taught both French and German, while others taught Latin. In his view, these subjects were too demanding for children who failed to master the English Language. He saw Spanish as more relevant to Jamaica than French. He pointed out the need for teaching the history of Jamaica instead of Greek and Roman History. At the same time he noted the deficiency in Science teaching and the lack of provision for teaching Music and Physical Training. It was to be expected that schools which were geared to examinations, and which would be judged by their performance in examinations would have spared little, if any time at all, for non-examination subjects.

One of the main weaknesses of the system pointed out by Piggott was the poor quality of teachers. He noted that fifty per cent of them lacked the required qualification. Referring to Jamaica's dependence on foreign teachers, he said that that should be a short term measure. He recommended that in the long run Jamaica should plan to provide her own teachers. This is still advice to be heeded. He suggested that girls be encouraged to enter Secondary School teaching because they made better teachers than men and they were from a better social level. They should be given scholarships to universities and bonded to teach in the island for a given period.

Piggott affirmed the importance of the teacher when he wrote:

It would be well to point out that the question of the proper staffing of schools is vital and fundamental. In comparison, all other considerations such as the sufficiency of school buildings and equipment, the supply of textbooks and the arrangement of the curriculum, are comparatively unimportant, for the reason that a good teacher will produce better results in a barn and with the most antiquated textbooks and appliances, than an indifferent teacher well secured in the most modern and up-to-date classroom.

Following Piggott's reports, the Secondary Education Law of 1914 was formulated. It attempted to define and modify the curriculum of Secondary Schools. Secondary education was described as 'education which does not consist chiefly of instruction in reading, writing, and arithmetic, but which includes instruction in Latin, the English Language and Literature, Modern Languages, Mathematics, Natural and Applied Science, Commercial, Geography, Book-keeping, Shorthand, Drawing or in some such studies and generally in the higher branches of knowledge.' This description was to give secondary education a literary slant for years to come. It was made impossible for anyone to associate manual subjects with Secondary Schools when secondary education was so defined.

In the first four decades of the twentieth century a few more Secondary Schools were built. The Government built Montego Bay (Girls) Schools; and Clarendon College was built by the Missionary Society of England and the Congregational Church. A Deaconess High School established by the Deaconess Home in 1913 was taken over by the Diocesan Education Board and became St Hugh's High School. St Hilda's and Cathedral High Schools (Girls) in Spanish Town were established by the same organization. One of the most outstanding secondary schools of the twentieth century was started by Mr Wesley Powell. Excelsior, started in 1931, was later taken over by the Methodist Church. Some schools that started out as Preparatory Schools established Secondary Departments. Among these were Camperdown and Merl Grove.

The Schools that have been mentioned still exist today, but especially in the urban areas, small Secondary Schools appeared and disappeared according to the needs of the locality. Many of these schools prepared students for the

Cambridge Local Examinations, the Pupil Teachers' Examinations and the External Training College Examinations.

In as early as 1924 grants-in-aid were made to Secondary Schools on the basis of average attendance and courses offered. An annual grant of £280 was made by government for the provision of £5 and later £10 Scholarships to these schools. Children in parishes without Secondary Schools must have had difficulty in obtaining secondary education as in 1926 special scholarships were created for them. The parishes, including Clarendon, St Mary, Trelawny, and St Thomas, were referred to as unprovided centres.

In 1941, grants to Secondary Schools were based on the grade of the school and the average attendance of the previous year. Two grades of school were created. Schools with an average attendance of at least sixty pupils, and offering courses for the Cambridge School Certificate to at least ten per cent of its students as well as the Higher Schools Certificate Course, were placed in the First Grade. Schools with an average attendance of at least thirty pupils, and offering Junior and Senior Cambridge School Certificate courses, were placed in the Second Grade. First Grade Schools earned grants of £6 per unit of average attendance while Second Grade Schools earned £4 10s. No grants were payable for pupils under ten years or those over eighteen years. Furthermore, the recognition of schools for aid was influenced by the condition of the buildings, fees, adequacy of teachers in number and qualifications, governing body, length of pupils' school life, and the emoluments of teachers. These conditions made it difficult for some schools to become grant-aided. But this did not prevent them from continuing their operations as private schools. It was S. A Hammond who recommended that a committee be appointed to inquire into secondary education. The appointment was made in 1943 and the committee was chaired by Professor Kandel of Teachers' College, Columbia University. Among the other members were Mrs R. W. Meredith who became Principal of Shortwood Teachers' College and Mr P. M. Sherlock who became Vice Chancellor of the University of the West Indies.

In the terms of reference, the Committee was required to investigate the relation of secondary education to elementary education on the one hand and to specialized and higher education on the other. Employment opportunities open to those completing secondary education were also to be investigated. Recommendations concerning the control, curriculum and staffing of Secondary Schools as well as the utilization of Secondary Schools to supply Elementary School Teachers were to be made.

Up to the end of the 1940s, there was no unity in the control of education in Jamaica. Elementary and teacher education was supervised by the Department of Education, while secondary education was under the control of the Schools Commission. The Board of Education was the advisory body to the Department of Education. Kandel pointed out the need for a single authority to control both elementary and secondary education. He suggested that schools be classified as Primary and Post-Primary instead of Elementary and Secondary. Transfer should be made easy from one type of Post-Primary School to another, and a wider variety of Post-Primary Schools should be instituted. To facilitate this move, Kandel suggested that a Common Examination be held for children at the age of twelve years to discover their ability for post-primary education. On the matter of private secondary schools he suggested that they should operate on government licence and be subject to government inspection. Concerning the method of grants-in-aid to Secondary Schools, Kandel disagreed with the bases used, and suggested that grants be made according to the needs of the schools. He saw no relation between the Jamaican environment and the curriculum of the Secondary School, as the latter was defined by law and had examinations as its objective. The need for a larger supervisory staff in education to conduct conferences, improve organization and teaching, was pointed out. Quite a number of Kandel's recommendations have been implemented to date.

The term Post-Primary was applied to Secondary and Senior Schools in 1944. The latter schools accommodated children of twelve years and over, and placed great priority on practical subjects. In 1953 two Senior Schools, Kingston and May Pen, were equipped to prepare students for the Cambridge Local Examinations. They performed successfully.

At the administrative level, the Board of Education and the Jamaica Schools Commission were replaced by the Central Education Authority in 1951. This body advised the Minister of Education who replaced the Director of Education, on both primary and post-primary education. In 1956, it was renamed the Educational Advisory Council. On the technical side, a Chief Inspector was appointed for Primary Schools and one for Post-Primary Schools. Under the 1957–67 National Plan, new schools were built, aid to others increased and some private schools qualified for recognition.

Up to 1957, each school conducted its own entrance examination. In 1958, these examinations were replaced by one Common Entrance Examination taken between the ages of eleven and twelve years. On the result of this examination scholarships and grant places were offered to Grant-in-Aid Secondary Schools. The Awards included twelve Code Scholarships and Ten Scholarships for Unprovided Centres. Annual scholarships were offered to children of thirteen and sixteen years old who came highest in the Second and Third Jamaica Local Examinations. This move began the expansion of secondary education, and the opening of the doors of Secondary Schools to children of the poorer class.

Indirectly, the recommendation to make Secondary School education a pre-condition for teacher training was gradually gaining recognition. With more students entering Secondary Schools, it was inevitable that more Secondary School graduates would enter teaching. The 1957–67 period saw the improvement of secondary education. In the area of curricular development, technical wings were attached to some Grammar Schools, and laboratory facilities provided. In 1946 Claredon College and Knox College took the lead among Grammar Schools and started teaching Agriculture. Business Education began to get some attention in Secondary Schools and the College of Arts, Science and Technology, and Kingston Technical School, which for many years was the only Technical School in the island, was expanded. Two Practical Training Centres, Holmwood and Dinthill, were converted into Technical Schools, and three new Technical Schools, St Andrew, Vere and St Elizabeth, were established.

The provision of Junior Secondary Schools since 1966 has greatly increased the number of free Secondary School places, but the need is still only partially met.

V

Teacher education

Schools set up in Jamaica prior to emancipation were operated mainly by missionaries or teachers from England. As early as 1832, the Moravians saw the need for locally trained teachers. A school for destitute girls was established and these girls achieved a sufficiently high level of literacy to serve as teachers in Moravian Schools.

The British Parliament also recognized the need for locally trained teachers. This they showed by earmarking £5,000 of the Negro Education Grant for teacher training. Following this gesture, a number of denominational Normal Schools sprang up to train teachers for their respective schools. These are mentioned hereunder:

Year	Denomination	Normal School
1839	Moravian	Fairfield
1861	Moravian	Bethabara
1836	Anglicans	Kingston Training Establishment
1839	Anglicans	Montego Bay
1835	Christian Missionary Society	Airy Mount
1836	Baptist	Metropolitan Spanish Town

Year	Denomination	Normal School
1837	Baptist	Montego Bay
1837	Baptist	Suffield
1840	Baptist	Calabar
1841	Baptist	Kettering
1842	Weslyan	Knight Street
1844	Presbyterian	Academy (formerly Bonham Spring 1841)
1843	Presbyterian	Private Seminary operated by John Aulds

In establishing schools the missionary societies were concerned not only with educating the negro population, but in christianizing them according to their faith. Therefore teachers in the schools had to be of a faith similar to that of the denominations that they served. All Normal Schools offered Reading, Writing, Arithmetic and Psalmody. Additional subjects varied from denomination to denomination. The Presbyterians emphasized the Classics and Mathematics while the Wesleyans paid attention to Methodology. The Moravians with their emphasis on practical work introduced Agriculture at Fairfield. In doing this, they were satisfying the desire of the Assembly and the Metropolitan Government for the teaching of Agriculture to be emphasized in schools. These Normal Schools had small student populations, and in the beginning the period of training did not exceed six months.

One of the notable contributions to teacher-training in Jamaica was made by the Mico Charity in 1836. They established three Normal Schools, one in each county. Two of these were of short duration. The third, situated in Kingston, has developed over the years to become the leading Training College in Jamaica. Unlike the other

Normal Schools of the period Mico was non-denominational. In its early years entrants to the Mico were required to write tolerably, read fluently, spell correctly and have a knowledge of the fundamental rules of Arithmetic, outlines of Scriptural History, and the rudiments of English Grammar. The courses offered were rather elaborate for students who had an inadequate elementary education. Among them were Sacred and Universal History, Elements of Astronomy, Etymology and the higher branches of Arithmetic.

The government's entry into teacher-training did not take place until after the termination of the Negro Education Grant. In an attempt to promote the teaching of industrial subjects, the government established a Normal School of Industry at Spanish Town in 1847. This move was to provide teachers of Agriculture in Elementary Schools. Contrary to its objectives, the school seemed to have given more attention to Latin, Algebra, Greek and Euclid than to agricultural subjects. It was closed in 1852 because of inadequate financial resources.

Resulting from a recommendation of Inspector Savage, a second Government Training College was established at Stony Hill in 1870 for training industrial schoolmasters. This was with a view to fostering the teaching of industrial subjects. A similar curricular pattern to that of the first Industrial Normal School was followed. On account of its declining effectiveness the school was closed in 1890.

During the period of Crown Colony Government, the authorities were concerned about the poor quality of teachers. In an attempt to improve this situation, Model Schools were introduced. They were used as Demonstration Schools and at the same time provided training facilities for prospective teachers. Owing to the difficulty of attracting model masters from England, they were of short duration.

The pupil teacher system

It was the failure of the Normal Schools to produce enough teachers that fostered the growth of the pupil teacher system, which began in 1877. A prospective pupil teacher was required to reach Standard Five of the Elementary School, six months before his appointment. He had to be in the age group thirteen to seventeen years and show an aptitude for teaching.

A pupil teacher was expected to assist in teaching and at the same time improve his academic status. Principals of schools were required to arrange special classes for pupil teachers and the former were paid for this assignment up to 1920. Written examinations for pupil teachers were introduced in 1882. Subsequently, Examination Centres were set up in various parts of the island. In addition to pupil teachers, volunteer candidates were accepted for the pupil teachers' examination in 1887. While these candidates paid an exam fee of two shillings and sixpence (2s. 6d.), the pupil teachers paid no fees. Until 1902 when a preliminary year was introduced, the exams were offered at the first, second and third year levels.

The curriculum for the pupil teachers' earliest examinations included Reading and Recitation, Writing and English, Arithmetic, Elementary Science and Agriculture, Geography, History, Drawing and Manual Occupations, Scripture and Teaching. The last mentioned subject was offered at all levels, except the preliminary one.

All inquiries into the education system commented unfavourably about the pupil teacher system. Teachers and educators pointed out the weakness of the system.

45

Resolutions from the Jamaica Union of Teachers for improvement in the system met with little success. S. A. Hammond described the term 'pupil teacher system' as a misnomer for what was involved in the system. He said this because the number of volunteer candidates always exceeded that of pupil teachers. Furthermore, the pupil teachers' qualification was used for entry not only to teaching but also to Nursing, the Police Force and the post of Sanitary Inspector.

The pupil teachers' examination system underwent minor changes in the 1930s. As a result of Hammond's recommendations, the preliminary examination was abandoned. Later, the Pupil Teachers' Examination was replaced by the Jamaica Local Examinations. The pupil teacher, too, was replaced by the probationer whose entry qualification was the Third Jamaica Local Examination.

In 1964, the Jamaica Local Examinations were replaced by the Jamaica Certificate Examination. This was a subject examination. In order to obtain a pass in the Pupil Teachers' and the Jamaica Local Examinations, candidates had to pass all subjects. In the Jamaica Certificate Examination passes were reckoned on a subject basis. The examination was renamed the Jamaica School Certificate in 1965. This change in name was to avoid confusion with the General Certificate of Education offered by the Overseas Examination Committee.

Teacher training in the twentieth century
An inquiry into the education system by Judge Lumb in 1898 criticized the training of teachers. As a means of increasing teacher training facilities, he suggested that Shortwood College, built by the government in 1885, be expanded, and that government aid be given to Mico and

the other Denominational Colleges. He also recommended that the duration of the college courses be reduced from three to two years to increase the number of trained teachers.

He found the curriculum overweighted with subjects that would not be relevant to the teachers' performance after they left college. Consequently, he suggested the removal of these subjects from the curriculum. Among them were Elocution, Latin, French, Algebra, Euclid and Mechanics. Practical subjects were to be introduced into the curriculum and School Management was to be given additional hours. He suggested that Shortwood College should include Domestic Subjects in its curriculum. This subject was already being studied by students at Bethlehem College.

With the incidence of a high proportion of untrained teachers, Lumb suggested the introduction of In-Service Teacher Training Courses and the institution of supplementary courses for teachers who were intended for special positions.

Certification of teachers was made dependent on success at various levels of the Training College Examination. Lumb recommended that the process should be simplified, so that the teacher's name would remain on the register once he was certificated.

The end of the nineteenth century was one of economic depression. Contrary to Lumb's recommendation that government aid be given to the denominational colleges, many of these colleges had to be closed. St Joseph's, established by the Franciscan Sisters of Alleghany, New York in 1897, and Bethlehem, were the ones that survived into the twentieth century.

Many of Lumb's recommendations were repeated by

the 1926 Legislative Council Committee on education. The need for the inclusion of practical subjects in the training college curriculum, the provision of In-Service Training, and Refresher Courses for teachers was stressed. In addition, members of the committee felt that teacher quality could be improved by the appointment of supervisors and supervisory teachers in the schools. It was recommended too, that a Domestic Science tutor and a kindergarten mistress be added to the staff of Shortwood College to facilitate the training of teachers in those areas. In contradiction to Lumb's recommendation, the 1926 Committee suggested the withdrawal of government aid from the Denominational Colleges and the development of Shortwood as the sole female training college.

Reporting in 1930, Hammond showed that none of the 1926 Committee's report regarding teacher training was effected. He described the training college curriculum as unrelated to the needs of the schools and the standard of the students who entered College. He repeated the need for training of kindergarten teachers, and recommended the institution of Specialist Teachers' Courses in Gardening, Physical Education, Handicraft and Methodology. He pointed out the low educational standard of pupil teachers, and the fact that they had no opportunity for improvement.

It is evident that no steps were taken to implement Hammond's recommendations as eight years later Lord Moyne found the training of teachers defective or non-existent. He repeated Hammonds' recommendations for supervisory teachers and Refresher Courses. He further suggested that the training college curriculum be enriched by making Hygiene, Physical Training, Domestic Science, Handicraft, Gardening, and Elementary Botany compulsory.

In 1941, Hammond, then Adviser to the Comptroller of Colonial Development and Welfare in the West Indies, criticized the way in which teacher-training was combined with schooling. He suggested that the latter be done in secondary schools with a two-year course for Primary School teachers, and three-year course for Senior School teachers. These courses should be combined with observation in schools. This view was shared by the Principal of Shortwood Teachers' College who in her report to the Kandel Committee recommended that teacher-training provision should include a full Secondary School Course followed by two years of professional training.

When Hammond reported, the Training College population was still a mere 187 students. On his recommendation, an inquiry into secondary education was conducted. This was the Kandel Commission. Because of the terms of reference, teacher-training was also examined. Kandel recommended that schooling for teachers be provided in selected Secondary Schools with a special curriculum the first few years. Provision should be made for the continuing education of teachers through regional conferences, scholarships, and the follow-up of students by college staff. The amalgamation of Shortwood and Mico and their removal to a rural location was also recommended.

Because of the island's limited financial resources, recommendations of the various committees had to be ignored. Following the Moyne Commission, however, Colonial Development and Welfare Funds were made available for educational expansion and advancement.

In 1945, the government appointed a Committee to

consider reports of the 1940s on teacher education, and formulate proposals for the training of teachers. In addition to the reports on Jamaica, the McNair Report on Teachers and Youth Leaders in Britain, and the Report on the Proposed Teachers and Farm Institutes in Trinidad and Tobago, were considered.

The 1945 Committee repeated Kandel's recommendation for the amalgamation of Shortwood and Mico Colleges and their relocation in a rural setting. Demonstration Schools and Experimental Schools connected with teacher-training were also recommended. The Committee further outlined the functions of training colleges. They were to offer two-year courses leading to A1 Grade, with a further year leading to Principal or Specialist Grade. Short residential courses should be instituted for probationers and those below the A1 Grade. The training colleges were to set and mark examinations for external and internal students, assist in organizing and conducting vacation courses for teachers, and select candidates for entrance to college.

Training colleges were accustomed to follow syllabuses formulated by the Education Department. The 1945 Committee suggested that training colleges should plan and develop courses and syllabuses in consultation with a panel of inspectors appointed to foster teacher-training. Scholarships were to be made available for selected teachers and administrators and the Scholarship Programme from Elementary to Secondary Schools should be expanded. An exchange programme with teachers from other countries was also suggested.

Of the preceding reports, Kandel was the only one that commented on the provision of teachers for Secondary Schools. The Kandel Committee suggested that the training colleges offer special courses for Secondary School teachers, and that scholarships be provided to enable non-graduate teachers to read for Degrees.

The Irvine Committee on Higher Education was appointed in 1944 to review existing facilities for higher education in the British Colonies of the Caribbean and make recommendations regarding future university development for the Colonies. In its proposal for a University College the Committee strongly recommended the establishment of a Department of Education. It was suggested that the Department develop post-graduate Diploma courses in education, research, set and conduct examinations, and award Certificates to training college students.

So far most of the recommendations of the 1945 and the Irvine Committees have been implemented though some have been tried for only short periods. The amalgamation of Mico and Shortwood was abandoned after much debate, and no action was taken regarding the Demonstration and Experimental Schools.

Colleges have assumed greater responsibility for the formulation and evaluation of the courses they offer, and the approach to the curriculum has been modernized, with greater emphasis placed on professional courses. Success in English Language and Education is now required for Training College Certification.

During the 1940s, a beginning was made in sending teachers and inspectors on study courses abroad. Supervisors of Manual Training, Domestic Science and Physical Education were appointed, and In-Service Training Courses organized for teachers. Between 1949 and 1957 Probationers' Courses were conducted at Mico. These Courses were of great assistance to those who were preparing for the External Training College Examinations. With limited accommodation in the training colleges, many teachers could be upgraded only through these examinations. Summer Courses, and Specialized Courses for teachers, especially those of practical subjects, became a feature of the government's policy in the 1950s.

The Board of Teacher Education was set up in 1956 to advise on matters affecting the training of teachers, administration of their examination, and award of certificates. By having representatives on the Board, the training colleges obtained some degree of autonomy.

It was at this time, too, that Moneague, an emergency training college, was established to provide one-year courses for teachers who had been teaching for years without the benefit of college training. Caledonia Junior College followed two years later, and provided a pre-college course for those who wished to enter teaching, or who wished to re-enter the profession after their names had been removed from the list of teachers. These schemes were undertaken to upgrade the quality of the teachers who were already in the profession. Despite provisions to upgrade these teachers through the External Training College Examinations, many teachers did not qualify because of the very limited time they had for study.

While the expansion of teacher-training facilities was proceeding under the 1957 Ten-Year Plan, a Committee was appointed under the chairmanship of Mr P. Evans, Education Adviser, to assess the teaching needs of the island up to 1967. In the assessment of teaching supply the Evans Committee found the training colleges too small for efficient operation, and recommended a minimum size of 220 students. Recommendations were made for the staff-student ratio to be 1:13, and the staff structure to include

Principal, Vice-Principal, Senior Lecturers, Lecturers and Assistant Lecturers.

As a means of increasing the supply of teachers of practical subjects, it was recommended that the training of teachers for Agricultural Education be undertaken in co-operation with the Jamaica School of Agriculture and that a technical teacher-training wing be attached to the College of Arts, Science and Technology. The latter scheme should provide teachers of Woodwork, Metalwork, Art and Crafts, Home Economics, Mathematics and Science. It was suggested, too, that the training of Froebel teachers be started on a small scale.

Since Evans reported, the former training colleges have been expanded and a new college, Church Teachers' College, Mandeville, has been built. College students can now opt for a Primary or a Junior Secondary Course. The latter follows a more specialized programme. The three-year Training College Course has been replaced by two years of extra mural study and one year of internship. There are no longer External Training College Examinations.

At last, the recommendations for in-service upgrading of teachers have been heeded. Since the mid 1960s in-service training of teachers has been undertaken on a year-round basis, and Refresher Courses are a common feature of the programme of the Ministry of Education.

The use of the Jamaica School of Agriculture and the College of Arts, Science and Technology as teacher-training institutions has been realized. Awards of Teachers' Scholarships, both local and overseas, and the exchange teachers' programme have all become commonplace in the education system.

Secondary edcuation as a pre-condition for entry to teaching has not yet been fully achieved, but a much higher percentage of college students have had secondary education than five years ago. It is now fully accepted by government and educators that educational progress can be achieved only with the adequate and proper training of teachers.

VI

Attempts at higher education in Jamaica

FOR higher education to be possible there must be an adequate supply of suitable entrants. In most cases, these must be people who have had secondary education or its equivalent. Prior to 1948, the inadequate supply of such people in Jamaica frustrated all attempts at higher education. Furthermore, the expense incurred in going abroad for such education has always forced West Indians to contemplate the establishment of institutions of higher education.

The earliest advocate of higher education in Jamaica was Rev. James Phillippo, a Baptist missionary. He envisaged a college modelled on University College, London. It would provide post-graduate and partial courses for those who had secondary, professional, theological and commercial training. Although the proposal was for a non-sectarian college, the professors and students were expected to be of high moral standing. It was suggested that the initial capital for the college be financed through the issue of shares, and that fees of fifty pounds per annum be paid by students.

Phillippo's suggestions were not accepted, but during that same year (1843) the Baptists established Calabar

Theological College for training ministers of religion. Commenting on the educational standard of Calabar Students in 1860, Dr Underhill, Secretary of the Baptist Missionary Society, found the preparation for entry to the College still deficient.

It was not until 1871 that the need for a college of higher education came up for discussion at a conference of the religious denominations. In addition, the denominations wanted the Secondary Schools to be sufficiently upgraded to produce students who would meet the entrance requirements of such a college. Following this conference, a deputation waited on the governor with the suggestions. These were passed on to the Secretary of State for the Colonies. After two years of deliberation, Queen's College was established in Spanish Town. Phillippo's suggestions for a non-sectarian college persisted and Queen's College was established on that basis.

The courses provided were in Modern Studies as these were considered appropriate for the country and the times. There were compulsory and elective subjects. The former included History, Ancient and Modern, Geography, Political and Physical, and English Literature. The latter included Greek, Latin, French, German, Spanish, General Jurisprudence, and Political Economy. Students could also choose additional subjects from Mental and Moral Philosophy, Logic, or Mathematics—Pure and Mixed, and Natural Sciences. This type of curriculum was chosen in preference to a classical one since it was felt that few parents would favour the latter.

The courses covered a period of three to five years. The three-year course took students to the level of the Degree of High Proficiency while the five-year course took them to an Associate or Honours Degree. For their entrance requirements, students had to be over fifteen years of age and pass tests in English, History, Geography and Arithmetic. Because of the disparity between the academic requirements of the colleges and the academic level of the Secondary School leavers, there was great difficulty in finding suitable students for the College. Some of the students who sat the Entrance Examinations were said to be unable to read or speak English fluently. Students who entered the College were unable to cope with the proposed course, and so it had to be modified. Unfortunately, the student population never exceeded three, and the life of the College lasted three years. It would not be unreasonable to say that the project was a complete failure as there were no graduates, and the college reached the stage where there were neither students nor applicants.

Several reasons were advanced for the failure of the College. For one thing, there was an insufficiency of suitable entrants. For another, the College seemed far removed for the rest of the education system. The denominations, too, felt that the public was not allowed enough participation in the running of the College. Staff appointments were made by the governor. There were people who felt that the standard of education of the College was so low that it could only function as a feeder for foreign universities.

With the failure of Queen's College, the government turned its attention to reforms in secondary education. A Committee, the Jamaica Schools Commission, was instituted to direct the reorganization of these schools. The first school to which the Committee turned its attention was the Jamaica High School.

It was not long after the reorganization of secondary education that Dr Nuttall, an outstanding member of the Jamaica Schools Commission, conceived the idea of developing a university in conjunction with the Jamaica High School. Initially, he contemplated a college affiliated to Durham University, England. He hoped that the venture would be financed from Jamaica Scholarship funds with additional aid from the Gilchrist Trustees.

The Jamaica Scholarship was founded by Sir Anthony Musgrave to provide assistance for deserving students of great ability who would benefit from an education in Europe. The examination was first held in 1881 and was of a similar standard to the London Matriculation Examination. Later on the Scholarship was given to the person who performed best in the Cambridge Local Examinations. The Gilchrist Education Trustees granted £100 Scholarships to some territories of the British West Indies for a short period.

After Nuttall's submission, the proposals for the introduction of higher education at Jamaica High School were drafted and later adapted by the Jamaica Schools Commission. Since the Legislative Council was unable to commit itself financially to such a project, the Jamaica Schools Commission acted as sponsor. However, a loan of three thousand pounds was obtained from the government.

Courses leading to the Intermediate and B.A. Degrees commenced at Jamaica High School in 1889. London, instead of Durham, had accepted affiliation with the College and so students read for London Degrees. In order to encourage local support of the College, students who came second and third in the London Matriculation Examination were offered Scholarships for the first time in 1887.

Students of the College were either from the Secondary High Schools or from Mico Teachers' College. Those from the High Schools worked towards the B.A. and

M.A. Degrees, while those from Mico did a year's course leading to the London Matriculation. The latter had to gain distinctions in the Training College Examinations before they could be accepted for the course at Jamaica High School.

In 1901, the College made a worthwhile contribution by offering a Scholarship to an elementary school teacher. By providing higher education facilities for teachers and High School graduates, the College was performing a much needed service.

Resulting from an inquiry into higher education in 1901, it was recommended that the College and the High School be called Jamaica College and that an Agricultural Branch be added. The use of the name, Jamaica College, became law in 1902. But it was not until 1909 that Farm School and Experimental Station were established at Hope. This was the beginning of the Jamaica School of Agriculture, and it was independent of Jamaica College.

The College ceased teaching in 1901, mainly because of inadequate financial support from the government. Of the thirty students who passed through the College, one received an M.A. Degree, four B.A. Matriculation, and several the Intermediate Examination. It was hoped that students would have been prepared for the First Year Courses in Medicine, Law and Science, but this goal was not realized.

While attempts at government level to establish colleges of higher education were short-lived and far from successful, many Jamaicans sat for External Degrees at London University. The trend started in the late 1880s and Jamaica became a centre for the London University Examination in 1891. In addition, Jamaicans who studied abroad seemed to have been rather successful. Cundall mentioned a list of 268 matriculating from Oxford University between 1689 and 1885.

Following the termination of higher education at Jamaica College, several suggestions were put forward for the establishment of similar colleges. There was a suggestion from Marcus Garvey in 1915 for a technical institute which would produce doctors, mechanical engineers, chemists and agricultural scientists.

It was not until 1926 that any suggestion for a college of higher education was made at the British Caribbean level. This was one of the items for consideration in the 1926 West India Conference. In that same year too, Hon. Nash, a member of the 1926 Jamaica Legislative Committee on Education, introduced a motion in the Jamaica Legislature for the establishment of a university in the West Indies. Three years later he laid proposals before the West India Conference for the establishment of a federal university in Jamaica.

A Committee was appointed to consider the proposal, but obstacles of finance and communication prevented any tangible move. One thing that came out of this proposal, however, was a request for Jamaica and Trinidad to investigate the provision of additional facilities that would be needed as the basis for the development of higher education.

In 1933, the Marriot Mayhew Commission on Secondary Education established the important relationship between secondary and higher education when it pointed out that the future of secondary education depended on the local provision for university training in the subjects of the secondary education curriculum.

While higher education was considered at the West Indian level, very little was done for other levels of education. The turning point came with the 1938 riots. Resulting from the findings of the Moyne Commission, a social and economic revolution was financed by Colonial Development and Welfare Funds. Higher education was ignored by the Moyne Commission. But in 1943 the British Government appointed a Committee under the chairmanship of Sir James Irvine to investigate the possibilities of higher education in the Colonies.

The recommendations of the Irvine Report echoed former ideas on higher education in Jamaica. For instance, the type of college recommended was a residential one in special relationship with an established University in England. As a result of this recommendation, the University College of the West Indies was established in Jamaica in 1948. Financial support was given by participating territories on a population basis. From its inception until 1962, the University College of the West Indies was in special relationship with the University of London, so that its students earned external degrees from London.

The following are some of the Faculties and Departments that have been established in recent years:

Year	Faculties and Departments
1948	Medicine
1949	Natural Science and Extra-
1950	Mural Arts
1953	Education
1959	Social Science
	Institute of Social and
	Economic Research
1960	Agriculture
1964	General Studies
1965	Management Studies
1970	Theology and Law
1971	Librarianship

Expansion of the University has taken place not only in terms of faculties and departments, but also in terms of additional campuses. Barbados and Trinidad have acquired campuses while other territories have extramural departments.

The institution of part-time and evening courses has provided the means of up-grading the qualifications of many Jamaicans who could not afford to leave their jobs and families to attend the University on a full-time basis. As nationalism grows from an idea into experience, the courses offered by the University become more and more adapted to the needs of society.

VII

Technical, vocational and agricultural education

Present structure of technical, vocational and agricultural education in Jamaica—1976

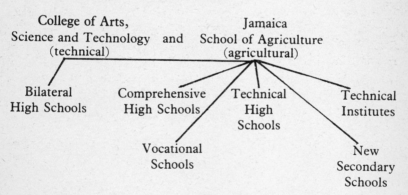

THE College of Arts, Science and Technology provides the highest level of technical education in Jamaica. It offers courses in Engineering, Building, Commerce, Institutional Management and Teacher-training. These courses are offered on full-time, part-time or day release basis. The College also hosts a number of short courses for the private sector and for the government.

The Jamaica School of Agriculture is the highest level of agricultural institution in Jamaica. It offers courses in

Agricultural Engineering, Agronomy, Animal Husbandry, Agricultural Education, Agricultural Economics, Natural Sciences, and Home Economics. These courses lead to a two-year Diploma in Agriculture or Household Science and an Associate Degree in Science (Agriculture or Consumer Education).

There are six Technical High Schools. Among the courses they offer are Building Construction, Commerce, Home Economics, Mechanical Engineering, Motor Vehicle Mechanics, Electronics, Agriculture and Crafts. All the schools offer courses on a full-time and evening basis, while two offer Day Release Courses. The Examinations taken are: London G.C.E., Royal Society of Arts, Union of Lancashire and Cheshire Institute, Jamaica Certificate of Education.

Twenty-one Bilateral schools and three Comprehensive schools provide courses in Business Education, Machine Shop, Technical Drawing, Home Economics and Agriculture.

Technical Institutes have been established at Port Antonio and Montego Bay. They are operated in conjunction with the new Secondary Schools, and provide pre-employment training in skills for young school leavers and part-time day classes for apprentices. Courses include Building Construction, Auto Mechanics, Commercial Practice, Electrical Installation, Machine Shop and Fitting, Carpentry and Joinery.

Knockalva Agricultural Training Centre started out as a practical training centre. It now offers courses in Dairy Farming, Farm Mechanics and Carpentry, Mixed Farming, Related Subjects, Animal Husbandry and Agronomy. Its graduates enter the employment market or do further studies at the College of Art, Science and Technology, the Jamaica School of Agriculture and training colleges.

The Carron Hall Training Centre for Girls offers courses in Home Economics, Crafts, Beauty Culture and related subjects. Formerly a Practical Training Centre for Girls, its students enter either employment, nursing, teachers' colleges or the College of Art, Science and Technology.

Trade Training Centres operate under the Ministry of Youth and provide useful pre-apprenticeship training for semi-skilled persons. The entrance requirement is at Grade Nine level and much emphasis is placed on practical work, although courses are given in English Language, Mathematics, and Civics. There are twenty-three Centres in operation.

Technical and vocational education assumes different forms at different levels of education. At the post-primary level, it includes courses in Industrial Arts, Industrial Trades, Business Education, Home Economics, Art and Craft, and Agriculture. At the tertiary level it includes Engineering, Trade, Technical and Agricultural courses similar to those offered at the College of Art, Science and Technology and the Jamaica School of Agriculture.

Attempts to provide vocational education in Jamaica go back to the beginning of the post-emancipation period. At that time the Colonial Authorities were concerned to make the masses in the colonies civilized by providing them with religious and moral education. Much emphasis was placed on reading and the study of the Bible. But there were those who saw the need for practical subjects in the curriculum. Among them was Governor Sligo. He felt that day schools should operate as schools of industry as well as provide for the mental development of students. A school of industry was interpreted as one that taught agriculture several hours per day. James Phillippo felt that in addition to agriculture, there should be industrial training which would include job training in trades.

The withdrawal of the Negro Education Grant was followed by a series of Colonial Despatches regarding education. A despatch sent to the Colonies in 1847 suggested the introduction of agricultural education. It was felt that instruction in agriculture should be connected with subjects of intellectual interest. But the Inspector of Schools in his 1847 report noted that industrial training was hampered by lack of water, poor attendance, and demands made on children by their parents. So seriously did the government view industrial training that their first contribution to teacher-training took the form of a Normal School of Industry to train teachers of agriculture for Elementary Schools. This School existed from 1847 to 1852 and eventually acquired such a literary curriculum that it provided few recruits for the teaching of agriculture. Fairfield, a Moravian Normal School, also offered practical agriculture to its students.

When the island became a Crown Colony in 1866, industrial education was given a great boost. Under the Payment by Results System, schools that spent three hours per day on the subject for three or four times per week were termed Industrial Schools and were paid one and a half times the grants of ordinary schools. Manual Training, Sewing and Agriculture earned extra grants for the teacher who included them in the school's curriculum.

The ruling class of the late nineteenth century felt that training in agriculture should be confined to the Elementary Schools since the children in these were destined to be workers of the soil.

It was a great surprise when Mr Solomon, Member of the Legislative Council for St Ann in 1889, asked the Legislature to consider the establishment of an Agricultural Branch at Jamaica High School. Although the request was not granted it motivated the Director of Public Gardens and Plantations to offer courses in the Rudiments of Agriculture at Hope Gardens to young boys. Mr Solomon's request was followed by several attempts by the Jamaica Schools Commission to include agriculture in the curriculum of the Jamaica High School.

The Commission did persuade the government to send Rev. Simms, Headmaster of Jamaica College, on a tour of agricultural colleges in the United States. On his return he got the School Commission to present a draft proposal to the government for the introduction of agricultural teaching in Jamaica High School. In reply the government suggested the establishment of Farm Institutes by local branches of the Agricultural Society since the government had no money for the recommended project.

When a Royal Commission visited the West Indies in 1896, it recommended the development of agricultural education and Research Centres where problems related to agriculture could be investigated. Consequently, an Imperial Department of Agriculture was established in Barbados. This prompted the Jamaica School Commission to seek funds from the Colonial Office to establish an Agricultural Station in Jamaica. The attempt met with failure.

The importance of including agriculture in the curriculum of various educational institutions was supported by the Lumb Commission in 1898. Continuation Agricultural Schools and Farm Schools were suggested at the parish level. The Commission felt that a knowledge of agriculture would assist people to participate meaningfully in agricultural meetings and enhance their appreciation of rural life. As far as Elementary Schools were concerned, it suggested that they should grow plants in boxes and pots where land was not available.

In its insistence to persuade the government to realize the importance of agriculture in the Secondary School curriculum, the Jamaica Schools Commission presented an agricultural programme for Secondary Schools to the governor and the legislature in 1889. A course in agriculture was considered necessary for those who were to be estate owners and employers. The establishment of an Experimental Station in connection with the Jamaica High School was considered necessary to enable students to study agricultural problems. The government responded by making plans for the establishment of an Experimental Station, and a Farm School at Hope.

Simultaneously with the Commission's request for an agricultural programme in Secondary Schools, a Colonial Office Despatch required the teaching of agriculture at all levels of education. Furthermore, the despatch suggested that training in agriculture should be compulsory for all teachers.

What resulted from the efforts of the School Commission and the Colonial Office Despatch was the establishment of an Experimental Station at Hope in 1901. Agriculture was also included in the Jamaica High School curriculum for senior boys.

Agricultural education in the twentieth century

In the early part of the twentieth century agricultural education was offered in Elementary Schools, Practical Training Centres and the Jamaica School of Agriculture. In

1906, agriculture was made part of the Elementary School curriculum, but declined after the Payment by Results System ended. Schools with at least one square chain of land were required by the Code of Regulations to have gardens. Two hours per week were allotted for gardening. In 1940, schools with extended gardens of at least one acre were given higher grants than the normal gardening grant.

The highest level of institution offering agriculture is the Jamaica School of Agriculture. It was initially established as the Government Farm School under the portfolio of the Department of Agriculture. One of the results of the Jamaica Schools Commission agitation for the teaching of agriculture at Secondary School level was the appointment of an Agricultural Chemist at the Government Laboratory, Hope. He gave lectures to small farmers, teachers and training college students. It was dissatisfaction with this project that forced the establishment of the Farm School. The School opened in 1910, with 25 students, and the number rose to 44 in 1913. Hammond in his report on Development and Welfare in the West Indies supported the transfer of the Jamaica School of Agriculture to a rural setting, and an increase in the student population from sixty to two hundred. The minimum entry was the Second Pupil Teachers' Examination. Hammond suggested that the standard of entry be raised to that of Secondary School leavers who could take Diploma and Certificate Courses. He felt that the course given should be related to that at the Imperial College of Tropical Agriculture. The transfer of the school to Twickenham Park took place in 1957 and the school was made co-educational in 1962.

The importance of agriculture at all levels of education has been realized only since the 1960s. It is now a recognized subject in most post-primary institutions and in the post-primary department of All-Age Schools. Participation is limited by the unavailability of land and the shortage of agricultural teachers.

Technical education

Technical education can be said to have had its birth when special allowances were given for the teaching of Sewing, Domestic Science and Manual Training under the Payment by Results System. Further development took place when the Board School, later called the Government Model School or Continuation and Commercial School, was established in Kingston in 1896. It served as a centre for the training of Manual Training teachers and its principal supervised the teaching of Manual Training throughout the island. Courses were offered on a day and evening basis in 1902. It later became a Technical and Continuation School and offered courses which led to the City and Guilds Examination.

Up to the 1950s this Technical School (Kingston Technical School) was the only one in the island. Vocational education was offered at the Practical Training Centres and through the Apprenticeship System. Carron Hall Domestic Science School was established in 1924 while Holmwood, Dinthill and Knockalva were established in the 1930s. Proposals for the establishment of Continuation Schools were repeatedly made by the School Boards and the Jamaica Union of Teachers. Although provision was made for them in the Code of Regulations, they could not be established because of lack of finance.

When Kandel reported in 1943, he found the Practical Training Centres still in the experimental stage. He said that they could contribute to the welfare of small farmers by providing the agricultural and industrial skills needed on the farm, but they should not be allowed to duplicate the work of Kingston Technical High School. He emphasized the need for more schools like Kingston Technical School in areas of population. These schools could meet the need for further education after pupils left a common primary school. As one of the advocates of practical studies in Secondary Schools, he suggested that Child-Care and Home Management be included in the Secondary School curriculum. Realizing the importance of research, he stated that the nature of the vocational training needed could only be discovered from an investigation of available vocational opportunities.

In 1949, a Technical Exploratory Committee was appointed to advise the Consultative Committee on Education on the aims, scope and types of the proposed new technical schools and technical education in Jamaica. The Committee considered technical education as a type of further education. The suggested types included a technical institute in or near Kingston, Technical High Schools near industrial and occupational areas, and technical departments of Secondary Schools. Courses should be day, part-time and evening. It was suggested that technical education be linked with apprenticeship in industry, trade and other professions. The Committee realized the need for teachers of technical education but pointed out that they would have to be recruited from abroad until the suggested Technical Institute was able to establish a teacher-training department. There was also the need for teachers in technical education to know their subject from the side of industry.

Further steps towards the provision of technical education took place in 1955 when the government applied to the Colonial Development and Welfare Department for funds to expand the Kingston Technical School, and consideration was given to the establishment of a Technical Institute in the Corporate Area. The Kingston Technical School was expanded by means of a grant of fifty-two thousand five hundred dollars, while another grant of two hundred thousand dollars made possible the establishment of the Jamaica Institute of Technology in 1958. Meanwhile, the Educational Adviser to the Comptroller of the Development and Welfare Organization and Chairman on Higher Technical Education was sent by the Secretary of State for the Colonies to inquire into the need of the West Indies for technical experts at the professional and sub-professional levels. He emphasized the need for artisans, craftsmen and workshop technicians as the first priority in technical education. He suggested that Secondary Technical Schools should provide a general education while the Technical Institue should provide part-time and full-time courses in technical subjects.

Private enterprize responded to the need pointed out by the Educational Adviser when Alumina Partners Jamaica Ltd sponsored an Accelerated Training Scheme for its workers in 1957. Following this move, the Minister of Education announced the setting up of technical schools in rural areas.

The government realized that in order for industrial expansion to take place, technical education would have to be planned on a national basis. As a result the Adviser on Technical Education to the Secretary of State for the Colonies was invited to Jamaica to undertake this task in 1959. He saw the task of the education system as that of creating 'respect for manual labour and the realization that without its accompanying skill and technique, a nation cannot achieve much in a modern competitive world'. He pointed out that a system of technical education should be based on general education, although subjects such as handicraft could be introduced into the early years of schooling. Like Kandel, he saw the need for co-operation between the teaching authorities and industry. He also emphasized the necessity for technical education to be followed by industrial training. The need for the objectives of the Technical College to differ from those of the University was underlined. Several changes regarding technical training were suggested in the curriculum at different levels of the school system. Among them were the following: Primary and Senior Schools to include Handicraft, Secondary Schools to include Woodwork and Metal Work in the first three years and Technical Drawing, Workshop Practice and Accounting in the fourth year. From this experience, students would be prepared for direct entry into the work situation.

Practical Training Centres should be renamed Vocational Secondary Schools. The minimum age of entry should be thirteen years and the schools should offer a four-year course. Kingston Technical School should be made either a Vocational Secondary School or a Secondary Technical School. He felt that the Jamaica Institute of Technology covered a wider area than technological studies, and so it should be renamed the College of Arts, Science and Technology. At the same time, the College should institute short-period courses for teachers. It was recommended that all the technical education institutions should provide further technical training through evening classes. Following these recommendations, Practical Training Centres became Rural Secondary Technical Schools and the name College of Art, Science and Technology was given to the Jamaica Institute of

Technology. Curricular changes recommended for the various levels of education were also made.

At the end of 1959 an Advisory Group on Technical Education was appointed to review the need for technical education in the light of changing conditions. The group included representatives from Trade Unions, teachers, the Ministries of Agriculture and Labour, the Public Works Department, the Hotels Association, the Chamber of Commerce and the Teaching profession. Members of this group were to advise the Minister of Education on the general development of technical, commercial and art education, the need for courses in management and industrial administration, and on methods of securing the effective integration of academic and practical training.

Between 1950 and 1961, the provisions for technical education were greatly expanded. Dinthill and Holmwood Practical Training Centres were converted into Technical High Schools and three others, St Elizabeth, St Andrew Technical and Vere Technical, were built. Buildings were added to existing Grammar Schools to be used as technical wings. The Common Entrance Examination which provides sixty per cent free places for students in Technical Schools was also instituted in 1960.

A survey by the Central Planning Unit found skilled labour in very short supply, so in 1961 Technical Institutes were established at Montego Bay and Port Antonio to provide training in trades and commercial practice as well as to upgrade the level of general education. Trade Training Centres were later established to provide pre-apprenticeship training. On a part-time basis, practical subjects were offered in Evening Institutes.

Further changes took place with the conversion of Knockalva to a Vocational Agricultural School. Yet the places in technical schools proved insufficient to meet the demand since in 1961 five hundred places existed for one thousand applicants. Despite the provision of the new Secondary Technical Schools to fill this gap, supply even now fails to keep pace with demand.

Since 1961 technical agricultural and vocational education has made great strides. Many of the recommendations made by experts have been heeded. But with the expansion of industrial development and the increasing realization of the importance of technical, vocational and agricultural education, the demand for places in these institutions still continues to exceed supply.

VIII

The management and control of education

Who controls education in any country does not depend only on the government's policy—it depends on history as well. Education in Jamaica as in all the former British Colonies was initially established on an ad hoc basis. The wealthier members of the society who influenced policy had little interest in education for the masses. Therefore no attempt was made to set up any general controlling authority. Schools founded from bequests were controlled by the Vestries, or by trustees elected by the voters of a parish, or by Anglican clergymen. When the Negro Education Grant was established, administration of education became vested in the various missionary societies. Although directives about education were issued by the Secretary of State for the Colonies, schools were directed by committees set up by their missionary headquarters in England. Applications for grants or dissatisfaction with the programme were directed by these Committees to the Secretary of State for the Colonies. With respect to the supervision of individual schools, each religious society evaluated its schools, provided textbooks and recommended teaching methods. The Legislatures were little concerned about education since they felt that it would cause the ex-slaves to renounce their lot.

In 1845 the Negro Education Grant was terminated and responsibility for education was handed over to the Colonial Legislatures. Following this change in responsibility, each colony emphasized a different aspect of education. In Jamaica, the Legislature gave priority to the provision of industrial education. A vote of one thousand pounds was made by the Legislature for elementary education in 1842 and five years later a Government Normal School of Industry was established.

A further advance towards the control of education was effected in 1861 when the Legislature set up the Board of Public or Competitive Examiners headed by the Anglican Bishop. Four of thirteen candidates who entered the only examination held by the Board were successful. The Board was responsible for examining schoolmasters and inspecting schools.

Education was one of the areas that received much attention when Jamaica became a Crown Colony in 1866. The entire system of education was overhauled and control machinery set up. The office of Superintendent of Schools and a Department of Education were created. This Department administered the Payment by Results System which was introduced to make the education system efficient. The Superintendent, later Inspector of Schools, was appointed by the Colonial Office, and was the Professional Adviser to the Governor on educational matters. In the 1880s he was made an ex-officio member of the Legislative Council.

In the first instance, the Department of Education was concerned with the inspection of schools and the collection of school fees. It was later able to classify schools and teachers. The Pupil Teachers' Examinations were introduced and centres established in different parts of the island. Aid to Training Colleges was also regulated. In its early days the Department of Education confined its activities to the Elementary Schools.

Major denominations such as the Anglicans and the Presbyterians had their own Education Boards. They attended to various aspects of education in their schools and expressed views on government policy. The Diocesan Education Board of the Anglican Church did valuable work in these respects.

It was the Royal Commission of 1885 that recommended the setting up of a Central Board of Education with the Superintendent or Chief Inspector as Secretary. He was to be assisted by nine Inspectors in supervising the Education System. Local Boards were also to be set up. Consequently, the Board of Education was established in 1892. The Superintending Inspector of Schools was made the ex-officio Chairman of the Board, and the other members were appointed by the governor. For the greater part of the Board's existence, the majority of its members were representatives of the religious denominations that owned a high percentage of elementary schools up to the late nineteen forties. Since education was the dual responsibility of Church and State, this was the means by which the religious leaders were given an opportunity to influence educational policy.

The Board had an advisory capacity but its influence varied with the interest of the Governor in education. Matters considered by the Board were sent to the Governor in Privy Council and then to the Legislative Council for approval. If accepted, they became law and if finance could be found they would be implemented. The Governor through the Colonial Secretary sometimes issued directives to the Board of Education to consider policy changes. Managers of Schools and later School Boards and the Jamaica Union of Teachers sent resolutions to the Board of Education for its considerations.

Duties of the Board of Education
These were set out in Law 31, 1892 as follows:
1   To consider and advise upon matters referred to it by the Governor.
2   To consider, discuss and recommend changes in the Code.
3   To consider and advise upon amalgamating and reorganizing schools and opening new ones.
4   To make recommendations to government about the expenditure necessary for educational provisions.
5   To mediate between School Managers and Teachers.
6   To settle cases *re* charges of misconduct on the part of school teachers or conduct of Managers referred to it by the Governor.
7   To initiate and prosecute inquiry arising out of any complaint or information received affecting the working of the Elementary School system in Jamaica.
8   To make and alter by-laws for the conduct of its business and regulation of its proceedings.

In 1914 the Board was given the additional duty of advising on changes in the Educational Laws and to report their proceedings to the Governor. The Board operates through meetings of its Standing Committees and Sub-Committees. At local level, Managers were appointed to administer schools. Many of the Managers were the owners of the schools.

Although the Colonial Office handed over the responsibility for education to the local Legislature, it still issued circulars and dispatches on education and evaluated the system from time to time by setting up a Commission of Inquiry. One such commission was set up under Judge Lumb in 1898. He commented on the composition of the Board of Education and felt that it should be representative of all parts of the island and have more lay-members. Members of the Legislative Council as well as ladies should be represented on the Board. He felt that the Superintending Inspector should be advisor to the Board, and the Governor, or someone appointed by him, should be Chairman. As far as local supervision of schools was concerned, he attributed the inefficiency of the education system to the large number of schools that one Manager had in his charge. The number sometimes stood at nine. He recommended that each school be given three members and that women be eligible for appointment as co-managers. Apart from visiting and inspecting schools, he felt that Managers should be responsible for the selection of competent staff and should see that children attended school.

For an education system to succeed, the interest of people at all levels must be secured. A move was made to involve local people in the administration of education by the establishment of fourteen Parish School Boards in 1914. Members of School Boards were appointed by the Governor on the recommendation of Managers of Schools and Members of the Parochial Board which was the Local Government Body. Parish School Boards in turn recommended the appointment of twenty-one District School Boards. Members of a District Board included the Correspondent, who was directly responsible for government schools, the Corresponding Managers, and the Co-

Managers for the Voluntary and Denominational Schools. In most cases the Corresponding Manager was the Minister of Religion to whose Church the school was attached. Visitors were appointed in cases where a Manager was not resident in the District where the school was located. Managers transmitted the educational needs of their Districts to the Board of Education through the Parish School Boards. The Director of Education as Chairman of the Board of Education and ex-officio member of the Legislative Council, was the avenue primarily through which local needs were made known to the Governor and the Legislature.

A Parish School Board included the Chairman, the Vice-Chairman, a Secretary and two other members. Duties of the Parish School Board were as follows:

1   To consider and advise the Board of Education on matters connected with Public Elementary Schools in the parish, especially those to be referred to the Board of Education and the Department of Education.

2   To recommend the establishment of new schools— Infant Schools, Infant Departments, Continuation Schools, Manual Training Centres and Schools—and the closing and amalgamation of schools.

3   To make recommendations for compulsory attendance.

4   To be the Board of Appeal in connection with the appointment and dismissal of Attendance Officers.

5   To supervise the general working of Government Schools, and act as Board of Appeal from the District Board in cases affecting teachers and scholars of Government Schools.

6   To consider reports from District Schools Boards *re* staffing, accommodation and furnishing of schools.

7   To negotiate with Managers of Voluntary schools when a transfer to a Government School is contemplated.
8   With reference to Voluntary Schools, to consider summaries of the results of the Inspection of such Schools.

Each parish had three or four District Boards. One member of the Board acted as Correspondent. There were at least three members.

Duties
1   To manage Government Schools in the district.
2   To appoint Visitors to report on building, sanitation and accommodation.
3   To perform duties assigned to it by the Parish Board.
4   To appoint Corresponding Managers for Voluntary Schools.

District School Boards had to be consulted before grants were made to schools in their district.

The responsibilities of Managers were very onerous and included:

The conduct and supervision of schools and the maintenance of their efficiency.
The provision of necessary furniture, books and apparatus.
The arrangement of school terms so as to get the number of sessions required by the Board.
Fixing dates of holidays and making all returns required by the Education Department. Supervision including visits to schools during school hours at least once per month.
Each visit must be entered in the Log Book and should

show date and hour of the visit, number of children present, number of children last entered in register, the date of such entry and the session for which it was made.

Arranging distribution of children where there are several schools in a district.

There was much dissatisfaction with the management of education in the 1920s. It was felt that Managers of schools were using the power given to them by the Code to discriminate against the employment of teachers who did not serve their religious ends. It was felt too that District Boards were unnecessary as they duplicated the work of Parish Boards and retarded the progress of educational matters. Furthermore, there was an outcry for a national system of education in which the government would take over the control of denominational schools.

The management of education was dealt with by the Legislative Committee of 1926. The Committee stated that Managers had in theory too much responsibility and so they ignored their duties. It was recommended that School Board be reorganized and be given authority over all schools. Inspectors were considered negligent in their duties. In order to improve the efficiency of the Education Department the following structure was recommended:

Director of Education

Deputy Director of Education

3 Chief Inspectors

Inspectors

9 Assistant Inspectors

Like Lumb in 1898, the Committee recommended that

the Board of Education should elect its own chairman instead of having the Director of Education as ex-officio chairman. The Secretary of the Board should be a permanent officer of the Department. Membership should include representatives from the Teachers' Colleges, the Jamaica Union of Teachers and three elected members of the Legislative Council.

Following the dissatisfaction with the working of School Boards, Law 11 of 1926 established twenty-one School Districts in place of the twenty-one Parish Boards, and forty-seven District School Boards.

The structure of the Department recommended by Lumb was introduced in the 1930s and continued into the early 1950s with slight variation.

In the earlier years of our educational history, secondary education was not recognized as a continuation of elementary education, but the latter was thought inferior to the former. While elementary education and teacher training were supervised by the Board of Education and the Department of Education, the Secondary Schools were under the jurisdiction of the Jamaica Schools Commission. The Crown Colony Government established the Commission as a corporate body in 1879. It consisted of a Chairman and five other members appointed by the Governor. Assistant Commissioners could be appointed as Treasurer, Secretary, Visitors and Examiners. Decisions were made on the basis of a majority vote with the Chairman having a casting vote. The first Chairman was the Chief Justice. Other members included the Attorney General, the Superintending Inspector of Schools and representatives from the Anglican and Non-conformist Churches. The Attorney General was included on the Commission to undertake responsibility for the legal aspects of trusts and to put its proposals to the Privy Council. The Churches had to be included because some trusts had been administered by them. As in other aspects of education, the Commission was established on the same pattern as the English Endowed Schools Commission. It was empowered to take over trusts and carry out a systematic visitation of trust schools in order to prepare and execute reforms of their governing bodies and make better application of their endowments to education. It also had the power to receive property and funds and to raise loans. As a corporate body, it could sue and be sued.

Special reference was made in the law to the property of the Walton Free School in St Ann. The Commission was to take direct control of this trust and use it to establish the Jamaica High School which would provide liberal education on a non-denominational basis, promote higher education, and provide free secondary education for a number of students. All aspects of the school's operation were decided by the Commission. These included curricular activities, admittance and dismissal of scholars, the system of examination, and even the domestic affairs of the school. Like most of the other trust schools, the Jamaica High School was a boarding school.

After carrying out the requirements for the establishment of the Jamaica High School, the Commission turned its attention to the appointment of new Boards of Trustees for the other trust schools. These Boards were similar to the District School Boards for the Elementary School, except that each Secondary School had its own Board. The Boards acted as intermediaries between the Commission and the Schools. Schemes were drawn up for the schools after their operation had been investigated. Although the Commission corresponded to the Board of

Education, it had financial and directive powers which the Board of Education lacked. It reorganized some trusts to ensure that their incomes were collected, and in 1890, it was empowered to sell trust lands.

Further powers were given to the Commission in 1884 when it was required to conduct Civil Service Examinations on which entry in the Civil Service was based. Through Archbishop Nuttall, its formidable Chairman during the last two decades of the nineteenth century, it was able to influence the development and expansion of secondary education. Among its important contributions was the drafting of the 1892 Secondary Education Law, and the Provision of Higher Education for a time at Jamaica High School. Like the Board of Education, the Commission had to send reports to the Governor and its proposals had to be subject to the same legislative process. When Piggott investigated Secondary Education in 1911, he criticized the absence of a woman on the Commission and the wide variation in the powers of Boards of Trustees as well as the inefficiency of some small schools due to inadequate funds. The Director of Education appeared to be the only integrating factor in education since he was Chairman of the Board of Education as well as a member of the Schools Commission.

As early as 1932, dissatisfaction was expressed with the lack of integration in the control of the education system. This caused the Board of Education to suggest the setting up of an Advisory Council to link educational activities. The need for integration was pointed out four years later by the Hon. H. E. Allan, Member of the Legislative Council. He suggested that the Schools Commission be an Advisory Board similar to the Board of Education with the Director of Education as Head of the whole education machinery. As evidence of the need for such integration, a Consultative Committee on education was set up in 1937. The Committee was required to deal with matters affecting education as a whole and members were drawn from the Board of Education and the Schools Commission.

The factor which made the government give serious consideration to the integration of educational administration was the report of the Kandel Commission in 1943. When Kandel reported, in addition to the Board of Education and the Jamaica Schools Commission, there was an Advisory Committee on Vocational Education. He pointed out that the difficulty of meeting educational needs was intensified by the absence of co-ordination between these bodies. His recommendation regarding the integration of educational administration was implemented in 1950.

Education never escapes when there are changes in political structure. So changes from Crown Colony to Representative Government brought about the creation of a germinal Ministry of Education and Social Welfare in 1944. As a result the Director of Education who performed the dual role of Civil Service and Political Head of the Education Department, was relieved of his political role. He performed his Civil Service duties while responsibility for education in the legislature was undertaken by a Minister of Education and Social Welfare in the first instance.

Following the recommendation made earlier, a Central Education Authority was established in 1950 to exercise the functions of the School Commission and the Board of Education. It was charged with the duty under the general direction of the Governor in Executive Council of formulating and giving effect to 'a comprehensive educational policy for the island not including higher education but having regard to the facilities for higher education which are available.' The properties, rights, powers, privileges, interests, duties and liabilities of the above bodies were vested in and transferred to the Authority. The Authority was a corporate body with the power to purchase, hold and dispose of land and other property for purposes of the Central Education Authority Law. The Authority's Secretary was appointed by the Governor.

Composition of the Authority

There were twenty-four members. The Minister of Education, who acted as Chairman, and the Director of Education, who acted as Vice-Chairman, were ex-officio members. Other members included representatives of Teachers' Organizations, representatives of owners of schools, two women, and five people from a panel of fourteen submitted by the Authority. Leading denominations were represented in the Authority and cognisance given to Kandel's recommendation by the inclusion of the two women in its membership.

A Standing Committee known as the Executive Committee and including the ex-officio members and eight other members was empowered to exercise all the powers of the Authority. This provision facilitated the execution of important matters without necessitating the meeting of the entire Authority. Duties and Powers of the Authority included making decisions on the appointment of the Principal and staff of Schools, and the setting of emoluments for teachers. All curricula fees and grants payable to schools had to be approved by the Authority. Changes in the Code of Regulations and laws necessary for the working of compulsory education were the responsibility of the Authority.

There were instances when the Authority had to be advised by the local boards. Such was the case with the appointment and dismissal of teachers. This could only be done after consultation with the local boards. As far as the local supervision of Elementary Schools was concerned, the island was divided into School Districts governed by School Boards of not less than three members appointed by the governor. Secondary Schools continued to have Boards of Management appointed in the same way. The Authority's recommendations on education had to be sent to the Governor before submission to the Legislative Council and the House of Representatives for legislation.

In 1956, the Central Education Authority was replaced by a statutory body—the Education Advisory Council. The Director of Education became the Chief Education Officer. Following Lumb's recommendation, the Director was excluded from this body. Instead, the Chairman and the Vice-Chairman were appointed by the Governor. The Council was advisory to the Minister of Education and the Chief Education Officer and had no executive power. The basis for selection of members was the same as in the Authority, but the Minister, like the Chief Education Officer, was excluded from membership.

Functions formerly discharged by the Authority were taken over by the Minister of Education. This was implemented by an Amendment to the 1956 Law in 1958 which made provision for the Minister to take over the duties in education formerly performed by the Governor. The separation of Ministry of Education and Social Welfare in 1957 enabled the Minister to assume full responsibilities for education.

Before 1957, the Director of Education was both administrative and executive head of the Ministry of Education as he did the work of Permanent Secretary along with supervision of the Education System. In July 1957, a Permanent Secretary and an Assistant Chief Education Officer were appointed.

The expansion of the Ministry of Education really started in the nineteen fifties, as can be seen from the following table:

1944	**1954**
Director of Education	
2 Chief Inspectors (for secondary and elementary education)	5 Senior Education Officers
7 Inspectors	12 Education Officers
3 Inspectors (Home-craft)	18 Asst Education Officers (A)
2 Supervisors Grade 1	3 Asst Education Officers (B)
4 Supervisors Grade II	2 Supervisors (P.T.)
2 Supervisors (P.T.)	3 Asst Education Officers (School Meals)

The scope of the Advisory Council's functions was also expanded to include the provision of schemes in connection with the management of technical institutions, Practical Training Centres and Government Training Colleges. Before 1956, Practical Training Centres and the one technical institution were controlled by Boards established separately from the Central Education Authority.

Further changes in educational administration resulted from the achievement of Political Independence in 1962. The responsibilities of the Ministry have widened to include not only the provision of educational facilities but also the welfare of teachers and students. Consequently, the Minister has been given general and particular powers in the execution of these duties. Among the general powers are:

the promoting of education of the people of Jamaica, and the progressive development of educational institutions for this purpose.

the framing of educational policy designed to provide a varied and comprehensive educational service in Jamaica and securing the effective execution of this policy.

the establishment of a coordinated education system.

contributing to the spiritual, moral, mental and physical development of the community by making efficient education available for the needs of the island.

The Minister's particular powers included the establishment, maintenance and assistance in maintenance of all types of educational institutions. Among these are colleges or other institutions for training teachers, technical institutions and training centres necessary to fulfil the requirements of technical and vocational education and facilities for further education. He is empowered to provide loans, scholarships and bursaries to facilitate further and higher education. Provision is made for the Minister to make available free places and assistance with books, and a medical and dental service that will enable students to take advantage of educational facilities. He is responsible for seeing that the requirements of teachers in public educational institutions are satisfied.

The establishment of School Districts and appointment of School Boards, the alteration of existing trusts and the creation of new ones are placed under the Minister's jurisdiction. He was also given power to remove the governing body of all schools. Under the 1965 Educational Law each educational institution has its own board of not less than seven persons.

Since 1965, the management of education, especially at the supervisory level, has undergone several alterations and changes. New educational institutions have been created and older ones such as the Jamaica School of Agriculture have been brought under the jurisdiction of the Ministry of Education. Assistance has been obtained from other countries and international organizations. These changes have necessitated the expansion of the Ministry and this has been done by the creation of new departments which inevitably is accompanied by an enormous expansion and restructuring of staff.

The diagram on page 93 shows the structure of educational administration in Jamaica in 1975. However, new ideas are likely to cause more restructuring.

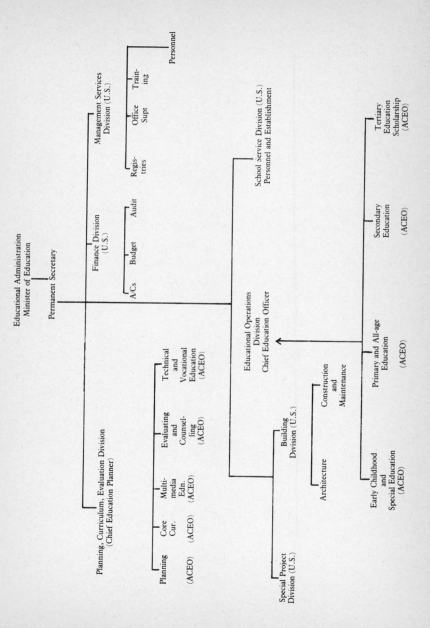

Educational Administration
Minister of Education

Permanent Secretary

Planning, Curriculum, Evaluation Division
(Chief Education Planner)

Planning   Core   Multi-   Evaluating   Technical
             Cur.   media   and   and
                      Edn.   Counsel-   Vocational
(ACEO)   (ACEO)   (ACEO)   ling   Education
                                 (ACEO)   (ACEO)

Finance Division
(U.S.)

A/Cs   Budget   Audit

Management Services
Division (U.S.)

Regis-   Office   Train-
tries   Supt   ing

Personnel

Special Project
Division (U.S.)

Building
Division (U.S.)

Architecture   Construction
                and
                Maintenance

Educational Operations
Division
Chief Education Officer

School service Division (U.S.)
Personnel and Establishment

Early Childhood   Primary and All-age   Secondary   Tertiary
and Special   Education   Education   Education
Education   (ACEO)   (ACEO)   Scholarship
(ACEO)   (ACEO)

93

IX

Development of Teachers' Organizations

Jamaica Union of Teachers
From your study of educational development in Jamaica, you will see that education has been provided mainly through the partnership of Church and State. It is not surprising then that teachers' organizations had their birth when each religious denomination persuaded its teachers to form groups. Regular meetings were held by these groups to bring about improvements in the profession and in the standard of education. The Moravians under Superintendent Buchner held their first conference of Moravian teachers in 1850. Later, associations were formed by the Anglicans and other denominations. It was felt that these associations could be used to promote the interests of teachers, improve efficiency and further the cause of elementary education. The meetings were not confined to teachers, and parents and Managers of Schools participated in them. Colonel Hicks, Superintending Inspector of School, encouraged teachers to form associations at parish level so that teachers could discuss mutual problems.

A boost was given to the organization of teachers when two leading educators from the United States were invited to give a series of lectures in Jamaica during the 1891 Exhibition.

A teachers' Institute was set up under the direction of the Hon. Capper, Superintending Inspector of Schools. Teachers of Elementary Schools attended the sessions, and benefited so much that they wanted the Institute to become institutionalized. The teachers' idea was reinforced by the experience of W. F. Bailey, Secretary of the North Manchester Teachers' Association. He was shown a copy of the Constitution of the National Union of Teachers (England). After reading the Constitution, he got the idea of forming a National Union of Teachers in Jamaica. He was supported by such men as Dr Gillies and Colonel Gruchy, Principals of Mico Training College, Bishop Nuttall and Mr Lindsay, a tutor at Mico. Colonel Gruchy became the first President of the Union. After a local meeting with teachers in his Parish, Mr Bailey called a Conference in Spanish Town on 30 March, 1894. Over 100 people including teachers, Training College students, and Managers of schools attended the Conference. As the organizer of the Conference, Mr Bailey was made the first Secretary.

As in other educational ventures, the lead was taken from England, and so the Constitution of the National Union of Teachers was adapted for the new Union which was named the Jamaica Union of Teachers.

At the outset, the union though intended for Elementary School teachers, secured the recognition of educators from all levels of the education system as well as from civic leaders. Honorary members included the Principals of Shortwood College, Jamaica College, York Castle, the Mayor of Kingston, Proprietor of the Gleaner Company Ltd, and the Lord Bishop of Jamaica.

The original aims of the Jamaica Union of Teachers were concerned with improvements in the welfare and professionalism of teachers as well as of education in general. The union provided for the formation of local associations where teachers could voice their opinion and take action in matters concerning their interest. It aimed at securing better remuneration for teachers and Benevolent and Annuity Funds. By improving the prospects of the profession, it hoped to secure better status and qualifications among teachers. It aimed at guiding teachers in applying for positions, and at helping Managers of Schools to secure teachers.

One of the first and most persistent resolutions at the beginning of the twentieth century was for an improvement in the system of calculating teachers' salaries and of grading teachers. This was achieved through the abolition of Payment by Results in 1920.

The Jamaica Union of Teachers came into existence at a time when government concern for the education of the masses was dormant, and the expression of the views of the public on education was at a minimum. Consequently, the Jamaica Union of Teachers had to use a militant approach to secure whatever changes it wanted.

Achievements of JUT

If you should look at the resolutions of the Jamaica Union of Teachers over the years, you would see that the benefits obtained by Jamaican teachers today were all put forward in these resolutions. One of the greater struggles was that against Article 40 of the Code of Regulations. This Article gave Managers of Schools the power to dismiss teachers for reasons unconnected with their professional duties.

In-Service Training, scholarships for teachers, and various types of leave were obtained through the Jamaica Union of Teachers. It managed to secure increased grants for schools, and to support successfully appeals for teachers made by Managers of Schools and parents. As a result of the Union's representation, the Inspectorate was reorganized to accommodate experienced teachers. Participation in the formulation of goverment policy was obtained by securing membership on statutory bodies in education.

Besides its contribution to the teaching profession and education in general, the Jamaica Union of Teachers has been a training ground for politicians, civil servants and non-teaching professions. It was organized at the National, Parish and District levels. Resolutions from District and Parish Associations were presented at the Annual Conference. If accepted, they were forwarded to the Board of Education which considered them and made recommendations to the Director of Education. The recommendations were then considered by the Governor in Privy Council, and laid before the Legislature by the Colonial Secretary. Where the Jamaica Union of Teachers failed to get a response through these means, representations were made directly to the Governor and in some cases the Legislature was lobbied.

Association of Assistant Masters and Mistresses
Although the Jamaica Union of Teachers had been operating as an association for elementary school teachers, there was no similar union for secondary school teachers until 1941. The Association began when a representative group of teachers met in conference at Highgate, St Mary. One

of the Association's first demands was for a uniform salary to replace a system whereby teachers were paid according to the wealth of the school in which they worked. At that time, most schools were privately owned but some received grants-in-aid from the government.

The Association was accepted by the government as representative of Secondary Schools. It played an important part in the Kandel and Hammond Commissions. Like the JUT, it was concerned with the welfare of its members and education in general. In 1958, it expressed dissatisfaction with the conditions under which overseas teachers were recruited, and later suggested the recruitment of Jamaican teachers and payment of their passage home. It fought for the granting of study leave, maternity leave, and adequate pensions for Secondary School teachers. It urged the standardization of the Common Entrance Tests and pressed for free secondary education.

Association of Headmasters and Headmistresses

In the mid nineteen forties, there were twenty-three secondary grant-aided schools. It became necessary for the headmasters and headmistresses to devise some means of coordinating activities in these schools. One area which needed cooperative action was that of sports and so meeting were organized for this purpose. It was out of these meetings that the Association of Headmasters and Headmistresses grew.

As secondary education expanded, attention was paid to matters affecting the schools in a general way. Among these were grants-in-aid, the curriculum, conditions of service, recruitment and training of Secondary School teachers, admission and entry requirements to Secondary

School, the expansion of secondary education, and the links between Primary and Secondary School on the one hand, and secondary and university education on the other.

Recognition was given to the Association when it achieved representation on the Cambridge Local Examinations Committee. This move provided the opportunity for the Association to recommend the introduction of new subjects into the Cambridge Local Syllabus. Through its influence, West Indian History and Geography were included. It was the Association that secured the change in the date of the Cambridge Local Examination from December to June. The step towards a Common Entrance Examination to Secondary Schools was made in 1956, when several schools held their Entrance on the same day. Two years later, there was one Entrance Examination for all grant-aided Secondary Schools.

The Association became the local arm of the Caribbean Headmasters and Headmistresses Association which was formed in March 1955, It was this Association that suggested the setting of a West Indian Examination to replace the Cambridge Local Examination.

Although the Association represented the Heads of grant-aided Secondary Schools, it saw the need for the integration of the various teachers' groups in Jamaica. This matter was discussed at a meeting in 1959. The Association was merged with other teachers' groups to form the Jamaica Teachers' Association but retained some of its identity in the Committee of Heads of Post-Primary Schools that was organized in 1965.

Association of Teacher Training College Staff
The need to improve conditions of service and the status of

training college staff and students forced them to form an Association in 1946. Beginning as the Association of Training College Teachers, the group acquired the name, Association of Teacher Training Staff, to accommodate members of the Department of Education at the University College of the West Indies, in 1959. Its main concern was with improved salaries but much time was spent in preparing schedules of work and in holding seminars to discuss educational problems.

In 1948, the Association agitated against frequent inspection of college work by the Education Department and argued for the right to set its own examination papers. It was instrumental in getting other teachers' organizations to think about an integrated teachers' union for all levels of education. It became affiliated with the Jamaica Union of Teachers through the Joint Consultative Committee formed in 1954.

Association of Teachers in Technical Institutions
This Association got its support from the Technical Institutions. It was established in the 1950s when the Kingston Technical School was the only institution of its kind in the island.

Combination of Teachers' Groups
In 1944, the membership of the Jamaica Union of Teachers was just over 1,000 although the number of elementary school teachers stood at about 3,000. There was very little inter-relationship between teachers of different levels of education. An attempt to get teachers to attend an all-island conference in 1951 got a reponse from elementary school teachers. Only four teachers at other levels of education joined the conference. Another

attempt three years later was supported by the Association of Assistant Masters and Mistresses, the Association of Headmasters and Headmistresses and the Association of Training College Staff. Consequently, a Joint Consultative Committee was set up under the Presidency of Mrs Dalton James in 1954. Although the Committee suffered from the pains of integration, it set up a Steering Committee to consider the possibility of Joint Annual Conferences, a Joint Magazine and matters of interest to teachers. The various organizations wanted to keep their individual identity despite integration. The Joint Consultative Committee did make its voice heard on matters of improved salary scales, point to point conversion and the change-over from School Certificate to the General Certificate of Education.

In 1961, the executives of the Jamaica Union of Teachers (JUT), the Association of Headmasters and Headmistresses (H^2M^2), the Association of Assistant Masters and Mistresses (A^2M^2), the Association of Teachers in Technical Institutions (ATTI) and the Association of Teacher Training College Staff (ATTCS), joined to form the Joint Executives of Teachers' Associations (JETA). This body was commissioned to draft the Constitution for the Jamaica Teachers' Association which was established in 1964.

Jamaica Teachers' Association

The Jamaica Teachers' Association is a limited company. Membership is obtained through the payment of fees. It accommodates teachers at all levels of the education system. The smallest unit is the District Association which includes teachers from an area within a parish. District Associations make up a Parish Association which meets annually and bi-annually. The Parish Associations make up the National Association which meets annually. Policy decisions are made at the Annual Conference.

There is a General Council which meets quarterly and operates on behalf of the Annual Conference. Among its members are representatives from various levels of the Association, trustees, coopted members, and Officers and Officials of the Jamaica Teachers' Association. The various levels of education operate as departments within the Jamaica Teachers' Association to represent particular interests. These include the primary, the post-primary and further and higher education departments.

Several Committees have been established to examine issues in education, and work towards the professional up-grading of members. Among them are Committees for Education and Research, Professional Development, Teachers Welfare, Salaries and Conditions of Work, Resolutions, Publications, Membership, Ethical Practices, Property Development and Finance.

At the Executive level, there is a Central Executive which meets monthly and implements the decisions of the Annual Conference and the General Council. Members include the President, President elect, one representative from each Parish Association and one from each Department. These are all elected members including the Immediate Past President, two trustees and officials of the Jamaica Teachers' Association. Further members can be coopted on the decision of the General Council.

Throughout its life, the Jamaica Teachers' Association has made a valuable contribution not only to educational development but also to national development. It has expressed its views on matters affecting sectors of the economy outside education. For instance, it sponsored 'Project Pull Together' which aimed at arousing civic-mindedness and discipline among young people. With the help of other national groups, it set up and maintained basic schools at a time when there was dire need for early childhood education. With the help of teachers from Canadian and United States Associations, it conducted Vacation Courses for Primary and Secondary School teachers. It initiated the In-Service Training of teachers on the job. With the assistance of Alcan Jamaica Ltd, it conducted a three-year training programme for Private School teachers leading to certification.

The Jamaica Teaching Corps which operated between 1965–1970 was begun by the Jamaica Teachers' Association. Under this scheme, High School graduates were encouraged to give teaching service for one year after an orientation course held during the summer vacation.

As far as conditions of service are concerned, the Jamaica Teachers' Association has gained improvements in Vacation and Maternity Leave, increased housing allowances for Principals, better promotional opportunities, reduction in the length of service that makes teachers eligible for pensions and increased salaries for all grades of teachers.

Through the instrumentality of the Jamaica Teachers' Association, a liaison office has been set up at the Ministry of Education to settle matters affecting teachers' salaries, grants, leave and tenure of service. From time to time, the Jamaica Teachers' Association has to settle differences involving teachers, school boards and the Ministry of Education.

In its famous Ten-Year Plan, the Jamaica Teachers' Association suggested many of the schemes that have been introduced within the last ten years to improve the education system. Among these are curriculum reform, the shift system, the training of all teachers, regional centres for training teachers, pre-school education, free education for 5–14 year olds, and variation of sixth form work to suit different abilities of students. Looking at the achievements of the Jamaica Teachers' Association, one can conclude that no obstacles are insurmountable for a united profession.

X

Post-Independence Education

After Jamaica achieved Representative Government in 1944, the growth towards political independence was rapid. A short period as a member of the West Indies Federation in 1958–1962 was followed by political independence. Each step towards political responsibility made the country more aware of the importance of developing human resources. As described by Harbison and Myers:

> Human resource development is the process of increasing the knowledge, the skills, and the capacities of all people in a society. In economic terms, it could be described as the accumulation of human capital and its effective investment in the development of an economy. In political terms, human resource development prepares people for adult participation in political processes, particularly as citizens in a democracy. From the social and cultural points of view, the development of human resources helps people to lead fuller and richer lives, less bound by tradition. In short, the process of human resource development unlocks the door to modernization.

The Ten-Year Development Plans after 1944 recognized and emphasized the role that education would play in the overall development of the economy. In 1957–67 it was stated that:

Educational Policy must look forward to the growing demands of an expanding economy and of our advance towards nationhood.

We cannot immediately hope to achieve the ideal theoretically perfect system, in which there would be free education for all children between the ages of five and seventeen years, but we can and must aim at something which will eventually give opportunity to every child in Jamaica, will make use of the best of our human resources, and will satisfy on a level of efficiency, if not generosity, the future needs of the country as a whole.

Throughout Jamaica's history, lack of funds has been blamed for the inadequacy of educational provision. It was fortunate for Jamaica that a change in the lending policy of the World Bank made loans available for capital development in education. At the invitation of the Minister of Education, a UNESCO Mission reported on the education system, and identified projects for its improvement.

Consequently, the Project 'New Deal' in education was launched. Under this scheme, an expansion programme for all levels of education was proposed for the period 1966–1980. The annual output of training colleges was to be increased from 350 to 1,000. The enrolment at CAST was raised from 355 to 766, and that of JSA from 170 to 500. In the area of student accommodation, 50 new Junior Secondary Schools were to be built for a population of 37,530 students. The Canadian Loan Scheme which became available at the same time, was to sponsor the building of 40 Primary Schools.

Some of the purposes for which the loan was slated had previously been recommended by those who reported on the education system. The education levels were redefined as Primary (6–12 years), First Cycle Secondary (12–15 years), and Second Cycle Secondary (15–19 years).

The inadequacy of Secondary School places had been pointed out by interested parties in education. As a means of increasing accommodation, Kandel had recommended the establishment of Senior Schools. At the time of the implementation of the New Deal Programme, there were fourteen Senior Schools. These were re-equipped and up- graded as Junior Secondary Schools. By the end of 1973, the 50 new Junior Secondary Schools were built and in use.

The Junior Secondary Schools have been designed to meet the needs of society by offering students a wide range of practical subjects, and preparing them for more advanced work at the second cycle level. Work in the Junior Secondary School was said to be equivalent to the first three years of the Second Cycle (former Grammar Schools). With the institution of Junior Secondary Schools, more places were made available in the Primary Schools.

Another feature of the New Deal Programme was the expansion of post secondary education. Any expansion at the primary and secondary levels of education would require an increase in teacher supply. In addition to the expansion of the existing Teachers' Colleges, Teacher-Training Centres were established at CAST and JSA. The former was to provide teachers of Business Education, Home Economics and Agricultural Science. The increased enrolment at both these institutions was achieved with a view to providing training for people in agriculture, commerce and industry.

Early childhood education for children of three to six years continued to be provided in Government Infant Schools, Basic Schools and Infant Centres. The almost complete absence of provision for training basic school teachers contributed to their low level of performance. It was an opportune moment when the Van Leer Foundation, a Swiss organisation, offered to train these teachers on condition that the government would take over the project after three years. The project was launched in cooperation with the Institute of Education, U.W.I., and as requested was taken over by the government in 1973.

As anticipated by the government, the number of Basic Schools has been increasing by sponsorship from churches and other voluntary organizations. Provision for further education has come through Evening Institutes, Extension Schools and the Extra Mural Department of the U.W.I. Evening Institutes have been attached to Junior Secondary Schools and Extension Schools to Grammar Schools. The former offer courses leading to the Jamaica School Certificate Examinations, while the latter offer courses leading to the General Certificate of Education.

One of the objectives of the 1965 Education Act was to provide an integrated system of education at the primary, secondary, and tertiary levels. With this objective in view, the supervisory system was reorganized to give each level of education adequate supervision. Many criticisms have been made over the years of the system of evaluating school courses at the primary and secondary levels. In 1966, an Examination Committee was established to plan and control the system of evaluation as well as to administer the various overseas examinations. However, this

Committee was short-lived. At the same time the West Indies governments were in consultation about the establishment of a Caribbean Examination Council, which has now been realized.

February 1972 saw the replacement of the Jamaica Labour Party which had heralded and nurtured the New Deal, by the People's National Party. Education policies are formulated by the legislative arm of government, and in a democracy, the philosophy of a government in power differs from that of the alternative government. It was not surprising, then, that while continuing the New Deal Programme, the government announced its new education policy in June 1973. It was named the 'Thrust of the Seventies' and became effective in September 1973. It saw Jamaica's greatest resources as her people, and went on to describe the government's programme to make people capable of serving the needs of their community and nation, and at the same time of raising their own living standards.

The most revolutionary item of the Thrust was the announcement of 'Free Education for All' from Primary School to higher education. In 1967, this type of provision seemed remote. Formerly, this privilege was afforded to Scholarship and Free Place holders at Secondary Schools, and Scholarship and Bursary holders on tertiary and higher levels of education. Free education meant that people would no longer be barred from educational opportunities through economic disabilities.

Students' Loan Bureau

As a further step in eradicating these disabilities, a Students' Loan Bureau has been set up to provide financial assistance for students in post-secondary institutions.

These loans are repayable on an instalment basis when students graduate and begin to work. Boarding Grants are also available for some students.

Conditions in Primary and All-Age Schools have been unsatisfactory for years. The 'Thrust of the Seventies' proposed to eradicate the unfavourable conditions and upgrade the level of primary education. Over a four-year period a programme for functional education is being developed for the first nine years of school life.

The Curriculum Development Thrust has been created to prepare syllabuses and guidelines in all subject areas as well as conduct workshops and seminars for teachers. With reference to early childhood education, the government has undertaken to subsidize eighty additional basic schools each year.

Early Childhood Education

Salaries of Basic School teachers were formerly obtained from students' fees. Since 1973, these have been heavily subsidized by the government. This move ensures that the Basic School children will have better quality teachers. A centre for early childhood education has been set up at the University of the West Indies to sort out problems in early childhood education in the Caribbean. The Centre produces teaching materials and conducts training programmes for teachers in early childhood institutions and personnel in day care centres.

New Secondary Schools

Since the announcement of the 'Thrust of the Seventies' much effort has been put into the area of secondary education. This is understandable since this is the level at which human resources can be most favourably developed.

Many Commissions of Inquiry on Education have reported on the absence of any relationship between school curricula and the needs of society. Since 1974 an attempt has been made to remove this problem by providing two additional years of schooling in the New Secondary Schools. The school leaving age has been raised from fifteen years to seventeen years and a Grade 10 was created in 1974 and became Grade 11 in 1975.

The Junior Secondary Schools have been renamed New Secondary Schools, and the Grades 10 and 11 programmes have been organized to prepare school leavers for the employment market, or for further education in tertiary institutions. Students enter the Grade 10 Programme at three levels:

Pre-Functional
Functional
Continuing

The Pre-Functional level applies to students who are unable to master basic language and computation skills. The Functional level applies to students who have mastered these skills, while the Continuing level applies to students whose competence in the basic skills will enable them to be prepared for entry to tertiary institutions. There is a movement from one level to another based on students' performance during the courses. A test in Mathematics and Language taken at the end of the Grade 9 Course determines the level at which students enter Grade 10.

In preparing students to meet the needs of society a

Core Curriculum Course and two Optional Courses are offered. The Core Curriculum Course is offered to all students at their levels of entry and include Language and Communication, Mathematics and Life Skills. Optional Courses are offered in Vocational Education and Continuing Education. Students who take the Continuing Education Course also study a Vocational Education subject.

A new feature of the New Secondary Education Programme is the inclusion of three weeks' work experience for all Grade 11 students. Assessment is on the basis of performance during the course and by means of a national exam at the end of the course. Every student who completes the course receives a Certificate on which is indicated his level of competence.

This is a rather revolutionary programme in the Jamaican education system. However, its acceptance will depend on the extent to which school-leavers are able to meet the expectation of employers and perform at the level required by the tertiary institutions.

Community Colleges
The involvement of the total community in educational pursuits has been secured through Community Colleges. These are institutions where people of any age or educational level can upgrade their skill and performance. They offer day and evening classes and provide courses from pre-school to pre-university level.

With a view to involving school leavers in service to the community, a National Youth Service was initiated. School leavers, especially those from Secondary Schools do two years of National Youth Service either before or after completing post-secondary education.

Teacher-training is always a crucial area in any programme of educational expansion. With Jamaica's inadequate supply of teachers it would not be advisable for teachers to be taken out of the system for training. Therefore, a system of In-Service Training has been instituted for teachers at all levels. At the primary level, a four-year course is offered to pre-trained teachers through Correspondence Courses, Month-end Seminars and Summer Courses. This is similar to the training college course and is intended to give full accreditation to those who complete the course successfully. The main objective is to up-grade pre-trained teachers both professionally and academically on the job. In addition Vacation Workshops are offered in all subject areas for all teachers. The Internship Programme for Teachers which had been under the aegis of the Ministry of Education from its inception has now been included in the programme of the training colleges.

With respect to secondary education, an In-Service Diploma in Education Course has been offered to graduate teachers in Secondary and Post-Secondary Schools. Another Agricultural Teacher-Training Project has been planned for Knockalva. The Excelsior Teacher-Training Project which started in 1970 with the object of training teachers with 'O' Level entry qualification and at the same time of preparing them for 'A' Levels obtained a grant from the government under the 'Thrust for the Seventies'.

The development of human resources in any country should be related to the development of its natural resources. From this angle, it is obvious that Jamaica cannot underestimate the need for training in agriculture and for devising means of making careers in agriculture attractive and rewarding. Therefore the inclusion of Agriculture Science in New Secondary, All-Age and some High

Schools is a move in the right direction. With industrial and commercial growth, the expansion of CAST and JSA and the Jamaican School of Agriculture and the addition of courses to provide needed skills will contribute to the fuller development of the country.

XI

The 'Education Thrust of the Seventies' and after

In continuing the development of human resources for an independent Jamaica, the production of an educated populace is pivotal. The role of education in political and economic independence has been recognized not just as that of transmitting skills, knowledge, attitudes and values, but as the key to the transformation of the society. Consequently, it is only through the removal of the inequalities of educational opportunities that pervaded the colonial system that change can be effected.

As early as 1957, the National Plan for Jamaica mentioned the equality of educational opportunities as an avenue to social, political, and economic reconstruction. With the extension of secondary education to more students on the basis of merit rather than ability to pay, the New Deal 1966 moved nearer to that goal. But equality of educational opportunities was made as realistic as possible within the limits of Jamaica's financial resources only in 1973. This was achieved through the proposals for free education implemented under the *Education Thrust of the Seventies*.

Following these proposals, an attempt was made to identify the needs of the education system more specifically. An in-depth study of Primary Education was made by a team of educators under the chairmanship of Professor Reginald Murray, the Dean of Education, University of the West Indies. In addition, there was an investigation into the feasibility and relevance of Post 'O' Level education through a thorough study of Sixth Forms. These inquiries showed that many of the deficiencies reflected in previous reports on education continued to plague the education system.

A narrative of the attempts to remove these deficiencies is presented in the following pages. As a means of reinforcement and in response to continuous evaluation of educational activities, the objectives of the *Education Thrust of the Seventies* were modified and, together with more long term ones, included in a Five Year Plan for Education (1978–83) dated December, 1977. A team including representatives from the Ministry of Education, the National Planning Agency, the Jamaica Teachers' Association, Jamaica Movement For the Advancement of Literacy (JAMAL) and educational institutions formulated proposals for quantitative and qualitative developments. These proposals were intended to equip students to contribute to the political, social, economic and cultural development of the nation and further the gradual evolution of an egalitarian society which would foster self-confidence, self-reliance, community spirit and national pride.

A change of government in 1980 did not change the education programmes that were directed towards the achievement of these goals. Universal Primary Education, the provision of skills training and facilities for early childhood education were designated as priority areas.

Unavailability of adequate finance is undoubtedly the major hindrance to educational development. The fact that the expenditure on education grew from $86.4m. in 1974 to $334.67m. in 1982 is encouraging, but yet there are still inadequacies in the education system which will be discussed later. However there have been improvements in many sectors. Curriculum reform and expansion in buildings have been undertaken at all levels of the system. The Ministry of Education was reorganised in 1975, and additional sections were established to administer the new services offered. Improvements at each level of the education system will now be considered in greater depth.

Early childhood (pre-primary) education

This level of education is provided for the age group 4 to 6 years in public and private institutions. Among the public institutions are Infant Schools and the Infant Departments of Primary and All-Age Schools, while private institutions include Basic Schools, Infant Centres, and Kindergarten Departments of Preparatory Schools. Much progress has been made in the development and co-ordination of Early Childhood Education since 1973. In September, 1974 a Five Year Plan identifying the objectives of Early Childhood Education and including suggestions for its reorganization and expansion was formulated. This was followed by a detailed survey of the distribution of Infant Departments, Infant and Basic Schools throughout the island, and the number of teachers and teacher-trainers servicing them as shown over-leaf.

Types of Institutions	Student Population	Teacher Population	Teacher-trainers
26 Infant Schools	9,885	272	
23 Infant Centres	869	25	
40 Infant Departments	4,887	105	
906 Recognized Basic Schools			45
1559 Unrecognized Basic Schools	95,898	2,437	

As public institutions, Infant Schools and Infant Departments of Primary and All-Age Schools are financed by the Ministry of Education and have trained teachers on their staff. But Basic Schools and Infant Centres are sponsored by community interests. They may be recognized or unrecognized by the Ministry of Education. In 1983 the former ones receive a government subsidy of $100.00 monthly for the Principal's salary and $86.00 for each assistant to supplement the fees collected from students. With such unsatisfactory remunerations, the quality of teachers tend to be poor. Therefore, the government saw the upgrading of Basic Schools Staff as its first point of attack.

In an effort to co-ordinate the training programme, an Early Childhood Education Centre was located at Caenwood, and the first training course under the new programme was offered to teacher trainers and representatives from Infant Schools and Departments in 1974. This course lasted for four weeks and included the development of curriculum strategies, the production of instructional aids, and supervision techniques. Since that time, on-going training courses including fortnightly workshops, residential seminars and demonstrations by teacher trainers have been made available to Basic School teachers. To intensify the training offered, Demonstration or Model Schools have been established in various parts of the island. The government provides teaching materials and a school feeding subsidy, and training facilities are offered to teachers of both recognized and unrecognized Basic Schools.

As in other areas of the education system, the Early Childhood Education Programme has benefitted from international aid. Community support in terms of financial contributions and management is essential for the survival of Basic Schools, but with the advent of free education, there was a decline in the community's willingness to continue this service (1974 survey). A Mobile Film Unit donated by the European Economic Community was used to launch Parent Education Programmes. This helped to mobilize greater community participation. The European Economic Community also built 25 schools, upgraded 75 others and funded university education for 17 teacher trainers.

The Organization of American States (OAS) is funding a Pre-Reading Project aimed at highlighting the basic skills to be developed before students are introduced to reading. This project is intended to aid reading at the Primary level as well. Since, according to the Five Year Plan, 53% of Primary School Leavers obtained low reading levels, the introduction of this programme should help to restore the reputation of Primary Schools as institutions where basic reading skills are laid. It would seem too that the Early Childhood programme is moving in the right direction since the OAS Project supports the idea of integration in the education system.

It is generally accepted that environmental factors are

important in the education of children. A United Nations International Children's Emergency Fund (UNICEF) project is being carried out in the two socially deprived areas of Clarendon and St Thomas. Several Ministries of Government are co-operating to upgrade these areas in terms of basic community facilities. In the schools, the quality of teachers, instructional aids and sanitation are being improved. The effect of these provisions will be assessed.

The major thrust of the eighties is in the area of curriculum reform. The present manuals used in Basic Schools were developed ten years ago when teachers had little training and so the manuals were teacher-centred. Now that the quality of these teachers has been dramatically improved through training, the manuals are being revised to make them more child-centred, to emphasize basic skills, and to promote child development through play. In order to encourage education through play, the Ministry of Education makes toys available on loan to schools.

Some degree of decentralization has been introduced in the area of teacher-training and in the distribution of materials. In addition to the headquarters at Caenwood, Demonstration Schools in other parts of the island are being used as resource centres, and training is carried out in the zones supervised by teacher trainers.

Between 1974 and 1981, the provisions for Early Childhood Education were greatly expanded. The number of Infant Schools rose to 29 with 1044 students, Infant Departments to 95 with 7668 students, Recognized Basic Schools to 1103 with 81,700 students and Unrecognized Basic Schools to 361 with 61,100 students. There were 7465 students in 106 Preparatory Schools. The number of recognized Basic Schools fluctuates because of the loss of status for recognition based on a minimum average attendance of thirty students. Furthermore no new school was recognized between 1978 and 1980 because of economic stringencies which affected the entire education system.

Despite quantitative expansion, the quality of Early Childhood Education is weakened by the high turnover of teachers. The low salaries cause many of them to opt for more lucrative opportunities, and those who gain trained teacher's status through the In-Service Teacher Education Thrust (ISTET) programme migrate to public schools. Much more attention needs to be paid to financing and administration of Basic Schools since they form the foundations of literacy and numeracy for so many of the nation's children.

Primary education

The In-depth Study of Primary Education identified and documented the time-worn problems of overcrowding, poor and irregular attendance, inadequately trained teachers, lack of equipment, an impoverished and unstimulating physical environment, all of which featured in past inquiries of the educational system. From time to time the government has stated its intention to eradicate these problems as finances permit. It was envisaged that over a four year period amenities and equipment would be provided to make the educational environment more conducive to the functional education of children.

In March, 1974, the country's 227 Primary Schools with capacity for 123,137 students had an enrolment of 143,726 students. 545 All-Age Schools with a capacity for 209,259 enrolled 280,175 students. The total teaching force included 5306 trained teachers, 5012 pre-trained teachers and 892 interns. On the basis of these figures, it would seem that increased accommodation and the upgrading of teachers were the areas of greatest need.

As a means of overcoming the problems of overcrowding, 17 schools with accommodation for 11,200 students were opened in newly developed areas, and the shift system introduced in 1972, extended to areas of high population density. During the economic prosperity of the late 1960s and early 1970s, several housing settlements were established to meet the needs of an evergrowing population. Provision for schools was included and, in some cases, schools were built in these new areas. One such settlement is the Portmore area, a twin city of Kingston, which had 3 Infant Schools, 3 Primary Schools and two Secondary Schools built.

On the basis of a loan agreement between U.S.A. and Jamaica, a Rural Education Programme was instituted in November, 1975. Its objective is to provide the type of education considered relevant to life in rural areas and supportive of the government's policy of human resource development. The programme was estimated to cost J\$18.2m with the government of Jamaica providing 55% and the rest obtained through a USAID loan for a 30 year period. An additional increase approved by the United States put the Fund at US\$22.3m. The five projects that are being undertaken include Primary Education, Continuing Education, Secondary (Agricultural) Vocational Education, Teacher Training, and Management. The first two are considered priority areas.

The Rural Primary Education Project aims at improving the quality and relevance of the existing curriculum. Six rural primary schools are carrying out a curriculum experimental programme in which teachers are given training in localising the curriculum. Plans have been made to renovate and remodel the schools where facilities are inadequate, and the possibility of school/community projects have been investigated. Under the scheme 25 schools are to receive diesel generators to provide them with electricity.

In the upgrading of facilities in rural communities, several schools have received electricity through the Rural Electrification Programme. A Canadian International Development Agency (CIDA) loan in 1974 provided for 24 Primary Schools and made additions to 6 other schools. Sanitation and other grants used to maintain the physical environment in schools have been increased, and are now based on enrolment and size of the buildings for all categories of schools. Previously, the size of grants was related to the level of the educational institution. Furniture and equipment are frequently replaced in schools, but the education authorities and supporters of the schools find difficulty in coping with the waves of vandalism of school property that started in the mid-seventies.

The inadequacy of school accommodation worsened when the 1979 June floods damaged thirty-one schools in the western part of the island. The schools remained closed for six months. This was a setback for the expansion of the education programme as money spent on the restoration of these schools could have financed additional accommodation.

The 1981 educational statistics showed the existence of 283 Primary Schools with 972,895 students, and 503 All-Age Schools with 250,149 students. This increase in Primary Schools, over All-Age Schools resulted from the transfer of grades seven to nine of the All-Age Schools to

New Secondary Schools which were built in several areas. After this transfer, the All-Age Schools became Primary Schools.

Irregular and poor attendance has always been a concern at the Primary level. It is too early to say whether the new thrust in compulsory education which commenced in September, 1982, will deal effectively with this situation. But to date, none of the measures used has been successful at the national level. School-feeding programmes, in some instances including the provision of breakfast, have had only temporary success. Compulsory Education Laws passed since the early years of this century have never been seriously enforced. Under the 1965 Education Act, areas within a three mile radius of a school could be declared a Compulsory Education Area, and some were so declared. These areas were provided with Attendance Officers who reported to regional boards.

A Survey in 1976 (at the time of going to press no more recent Survey was available) showed the following pattern of variation in attendance between Kingston and the rural schools:

Parish	No. of Schools	Enrolment	Attendance	Percent Attendance
Kingston	34	31,847	27,835	87.2
Rural Parishes	782	439,103	338,912	70.2
St Thomas	43	20,110	12,991	64.5

Another survey in 1977 showed that the work of the attendance officers was ineffective since no legal sanctions followed reports of non-attendance. As a result of these findings, the role of Attendance Officers was redefined to allow greater accountability to the Senior Education

Officers in their areas, and a closer relationship with parents and teachers in their work.

The Five-Year Plan (1978–83) stated that the average attendance in primary schools was 67%. This pattern of attendance certainly has implications for the low level of literacy identified among primary school-leavers. It was evident that the policy-makers had to find some means of improving attendance. So the first move in this direction was the extension of Compulsory Attendance Law in September, 1982 to the parishes of St Thomas and Trelawny which had the lowest level of attendance. It is projected that by 1985 the entire island will be under this law.

A new feature of the 1982 Compulsory Attendance Policy is the provision of lunch and clothing for children to facilitate their attendance at school. The students included are those registered in grades one through six. Provisions are made to deal with unco-operative parents in the Family Court and truant students in the Juvenile Courts. Penalties in terms of fines and imprisonment vary with the number of offences.

To improve the quality of the teaching staff, teacher training facilities were increased and a massive in-service-training of pre-trained teachers was instituted. A National Volunteer Service was used to assist the teaching staff in schools. It was seen by the government as an opportunity for those who obtained a secondary education to give the nation two years service in areas of critical shortages, and the first priority was given to teaching.

In the area of curriculum reform, the Curriculum Development Thrust was launched in 1974 with a statement of the desired outcome of nine years of functional education. These outcomes were used as guides in preparing learning activities for grades one to nine. It was proposed that work on two grades would be introduced each year beginning with one and seven, so that by 1977 all grades would have syllabuses and supporting materials. The implementation of the Curriculum Development Thrust saw a distinct departure from a system where teachers worked from syllabuses made by themselves or by the education authorities. Some curriculum reform had been taking place since 1966. People who were involved in Science, Mathematics and Remedial Reading Projects were invited to co-operate with teachers, UWI staff, and Ministry of Education officials to develop curriculum materials.

Teachers needed to familiarize themselves with the operations of the Thrust and to be aware of how they could contribute to the programme. This was done through conferences. Resource teachers selected from the teaching force received training to perform leadership roles in teacher's seminars. The Thrust produced hundreds of manuals and later curriculum guides for distribution to schools while teachers were prepared in one day seminars to interpret and apply them.

On-going tests of materials served to identify problems and lay the foundation for further revision as well as help teachers to recognize evaluation as an indispensable aspect of curriculum development. Although the people involved were highly motivated by the programme, the inadequacies of supervision and pretesting of materials mitigated against its full impact.

The restructuring of the Ministry of Education in 1975 saw the inclusion of a Core Curriculum Unit which absorbed the work of the Thrust. Since then the curriculum guides have been revised and placed in schools. Instead of large group workshops, small groups of teachers are given on-site training and more attention is paid to local needs.

Despite the foundations laid by the Curriculum Development Thrust, the Five Year Plan (1978–83) decried the poor quality of primary education. Although other factors were blamed for this, an integrated curriculum with emphasis on language, mathematics, and study skills was seen as the basis for planned development of attitudes and skills.

An attempt at supplying an integrated curriculum was the Language Programme Series grades 1–3 designed for the Jamaican child, and including readers, workbooks, story books, wall charts and detailed teachers' guide. Grades 4–6 series are currently being developed. The Project is funded by the OAS.

A Primary Learning Materials Project funded by the World Bank has now been launched to provide materials in Language Arts, Social Studies, Science and Mathematics. With skills training being identified as one of the priorities in the present education policy, primary education students will have to be assisted to develop the sensory-motor skills that will prepare them for the acquisition of vocational and technical skills at the secondary level.

In an era of change, new approaches in education are sought and tried. One such is Project Primer (Project for Reshaping and Improving the Management of Educational Resources) carried out in five remote rural schools in the culturally disadvantaged areas of Manchester. It is sponsored by the International Development Research Centre (IDRC) of Canada, and aims at studying ways in which the country can manage its educational resources more effectively. Among the ways studied are the involvement of the community in the education process and the allocation of a fair share of attention to each child in school through small group teaching. At the same time, sharing and interaction between older and younger children are encouraged.

Under the scheme, group cohesiveness is fostered through the formation of families consisting of grades 7, 8 and 9 students acting as tutors for students of grades 1, 2 and 3. Teachers are responsible for large group teaching and for guiding the tutors. Response to the Project which is now being evaluated is considered favourable. It might be difficult to use this approach in large schools, but it can be a means of coping with the inadequate staffing of small multi-grade schools so prevalent in rural Jamaica.

Secondary education

For many years secondary education in Jamaica has been synonymous with grammar type schools which offered the curriculum specified under the 1914 Education Law. Availability of this type of education was based almost exclusively on the ability to pay. The curriculum was geared to meet the needs of a foreign culture and to satisfy the requirements of foreign-based examinations. It is little wonder that the education offered was dubbed irrelevant to the needs of Jamaica.

Recommendations for relevance and some degree of variability in the education system were made by a number of commissions of inquiry ending with Kandel. It was the implementation of some of these recommendations that laid the basis for less exclusive and more relevant educational provisions.

Availability of secondary education to a higher percentage of the population began with the establishment of

Senior Elementary Schools in the early 1950s. Although emphasis in these schools was on practical work, two of them were selected to carry out experiments in the teaching of subjects at the secondary level and the preparation of students for the Senior Cambridge Examination. The institution of the Common Entrance Examination, first to Grant-Aided Secondary Schools, and later to Technical High Schools provided free and grant places on merit rather than the ability to pay. In 1964, two Comprehensive High Schools, Trench Town and Frankfield, were built in economically disadvantaged areas. In addition to receiving students through the Common Entrance Examinations, they received twelve year olds from Primary Schools in their vicinity. These provisions placed students from the lower socio-economic group into schools that were once the preserve of middle and upper socio-economic groups, and made secondary education available to a higher percentage of the population.

The New Deal Programme brought into existence the Junior Secondary Schools. The education offered by these schools was intended to be similar to that which was available in the first three years of the traditional High schools, but there were deficiencies. Instead of entry through the Common Entrance Examinations, Primary Schools in the areas where Junior Secondary Schools existed were designated feeder schools. Children who were not selected for entry to the traditional High Schools were transferred to the Junior Secondary Schools at the age of 12.

A giant step was made towards equality of educational opportunity when free education was included under the Thrust of the Seventies. This meant that all tuition fees, as well as fees for games, boarding, and laboratories, were abolished. The Junior Secondary Schools were put on par with the traditional High Schools in terms of the duration of the course, and became five year instead of three year schools. To meet the expansion in secondary education, the shift system which had been operating in two Junior Secondary Schools since 1972, was extended to four other schools. Under a World Bank Programme, provision was made for an additional 12 New Secondary Schools, 1 High School and 1 Technical School.

The decade following the *Education Thrust of the Seventies* has seen many changes in the structure, offerings, and evaluation of Secondary Education. In terms of numbers, enrolment increased from 155,901 excluding Independent Schools to 248,959 in 1980 with 9,444 students in Independent Schools.

Secondary High Schools

The number of secondary high schools increased from 40 in 1974 to 46 in 1980. Five independent schools came under government financing. They were Marymount and William Knibb in 1975, Campion and DeCartaret in 1976, and Bishop in 1978. One new school, Charlemont in St Catherine, was built. The country's economic resources prevented the building of more High Schools. So in order to satisfy the increasing demand for places in these schools, extension schools were added to some existing schools. This facilitated students who did not qualify for entry through the Common Entrance Examination. The extension schools were fee-paying and came under the category of Independent Schools. In 1978 they were converted into additional shifts to the schools which sponsored them, and their students ceased to pay fees.

130

Since the early 1960s, the Jamaican economy has been moving towards greater industrialization. The increasing demand for technical skills cannot be met adequately by existing technical schools. Moreover, there is greater understanding of the philosophy that the education system should equip people with skills necessary for the country's development. Consequently, more and more High Schools have been varying their offerings to include technical and vocational areas.

By 1981, nearly all of them were offering Home Economics, Technical Drawing, Industrial Arts, Business Education, Art and Crafts, and Agricultural Science. Such subjects as Physical Training, Music and Drama have also become much more important in the life of every school. Spanish, which Piggott (1911) saw as being more relevant to the needs of Jamaica than French, is taught in all schools, with French and German to a lesser extent.

Another change in the structure of High School has been the combination of some of them with New Secondary Schools, as happened in the cases of Happy Grove, Oberlin, St Catherine High, Morant Bay and Rusea's High. In each case, the High School and the New Secondary School came under the jurisdiction of one principal. However, the establishment of Community Colleges has resulted in some High Schools losing their Sixth Forms to these institutions.

Technical High Schools
Students enter these schools through the 13+ Common Entrance Examinations and the Grade Nine Achievement Test. Through a four year programme, they obtain qualifications similar to that of high schools. In addition, some Technical Schools offer G.C.E. 'A' Level courses.

131

Extensive agricultural programmes are carried out at Vere, Dinthill and Holmwood. There has even been an experiment in student co-operative farming. Day Release Courses provide training in vocational areas to enable students to qualify under the Apprenticeship Law. Evening classes meet the needs of the community for technical and vocational skills.

Technical Schools work in close co-operation with their communities. A new feature of these schools has been the introduction of 'Industry Day' when interested persons from the industrial and commercial sectors visit schools and discuss with teachers the preparation of students for job opportunities. On-the-job work experience has also helped to cement the schools relationship with these sectors.

Although technical skills are in greater demand then any other to boost the country's industrial development, only one technical school, Dunoon Park, has been built since 1961. The high cost of building and equipping these schools as well as their high recurrent cost seems to preclude their proliferation. In 1981, their per capita recurrent cost stood at $1152. Instead, New Secondary Schools, with a per capita recurrent cost of only $532, have been extensively used to provide technical and vocational education. At the same time, extensive additions to the physical plants of Technical Schools have increased accommodation so that between 1973 and 1981 their full-time population increased from 4251 to 7711.

Vocational Schools

Vocational Education in the formal system was previously offered at Carron Hall (Girls) and Knockalva (Boys) Vocational Schools, as well as Montego Bay and Port

Antonio Technical Institutes. The latter institutions have been absorbed into neighbouring New Secondary Schools, and Knockalva has been integrated with a New Secondary School to form an Agricultural Secondary School. These now operate as separate schools. Carron Hall was destroyed by fire in 1981, but there are plans to restore it. There are training centres subsidized by government that offer vocational education to All-Age School-leavers as well as drop-outs from Secondary institutions. These include Rosedale in St Andrew, St Ann and Westmoreland Housecraft Training Centres, Goodwill (St James) and Lucea (Hanover) Schools of Home Economics, and Young Women's Christian Association (YWCA) School Leavers' Institute in Kingston and Spanish Town. They operate up to Grade Eleven Standard.

Agricultural Secondary Schools
Under the Rural Secondary Education Project three new Agricultural/Vocational Schools have been constructed. The first was Elim in St Elizabeth which opened in 1979, and then Passley Gardens in Portland was opened in 1981. Knockalva is the third of these schools. The aim of the project is the full utilization of both human and material resources in Agriculture and Home Economics. Entrants to these schools are required to pass the Grade Nine Achievement Test (GNAT) as well as an entrance exam set by individual schools.

Agricultural Schools offer a three-year course in practical and theoretical Agriculture. The subjects include Mathematics, English Language, Integrated Science, Animal Husbandry, Animal Science, Crops, Agricultural Economics and Agricultural Engineering. Graduates of these schools are qualified to work as

Agricultural Extension Officers or as pre-trained teachers. In addition, they meet the entry requirements for acceptance to the College of Agriculture.

In 1982 Passley Gardens was phased out and students transferred to Elim and Knockalva. The physical facilities at the schools have been upgraded to accommodate the new College of Agriculture.

Comprehensive High Schools

In 1966, when the only Comprehensive High Schools were at Frankfield and Trench Town, a Comprehensive School was described as a High School, a Technical School, a Junior Secondary School, and possibly a Vocational School in one. These facilities are still available, and transfer takes place from one to the other in the interests of students. Furthermore, these schools are intended to embrace the concept of the total school and involve all members of the community, so that Infant, Adult and Community Education *is* expected to be encouraged on a voluntary basis.

Four Comprehensive High Schools have been added to the two built in 1966. A former Junior Secondary School, Tivoli Gardens, established in 1969, has been upgraded to a Comprehensive School. Three others, Charlie Smith (Jones Town) in St Andrew, Herbert Morrison (Montego Bay) in St James, and Garvey Maceo, Clarendon, have been built. They all provide a combination of grammar-type, technical and vocational education.

New Secondary Schools

Between 1974 and 1981, the number of these schools rose from 61 to 80, and the student population from 54,035 to 94,788. In 1980, 54 schools provided accommodation through the shift system. The New Secondary Schools have exemplified the principle of integration with the primary system by accepting all twelve year olds from their feeder schools. More than any other secondary institution in the country, the New Secondary School attempts to cater for the needs of the society as well as for those of the individuals.

In its curriculum, provisions are made for technical, commercial, industrial and agricultural training. Besides the subjects offered in a traditional secondary school, there are courses in such areas as Auto-Mechanics, Electrical Installation, Clerical Work and Merchandising, Hotel Services, Business Education, Food and Nutrition and Agricultural Science. Emphasis on agriculture is seen from the fact that the number of schools offering agriculture rose from 2 in 1969 to 75 in 1979. Some schools have tutorial farms ranging from one to fifty acres.

Students enter the course suitable to their level of ability and are prepared for entry to employment and to tertiary institutions. They are helped to acquire skills in Consumer Education and Budgeting, as well as proper work attitudes and Family Life Education. Cultural activities and guidance counselling are available to all students. Relationship to the world of work is established through work experience programmes. A more recent innovation in the New Secondary Schools has been the Production Plan whereby farm produce, furniture, metal work, clothing and textiles are produced in commercially viable quantities. These projects attract government subsidies.

Independent Schools

Although the government's education policy indirectly helped to reduce the number of independent schools, the

135

inadequacies of facilities in the public system have perpetuated their existence. The association of quality education with some of these schools, and the elitist ambitions of some members of the higher socio-economic groups contribute to their success. Many of them are sponsored by religious denominations whose role in education is traditional and still substantial.

They offer education from Pre-Primary through Secondary to Tertiary levels, and include the evening divisions of public secondary and tertiary institutions. The Preparatory Schools have both Infant and Primary Departments, and their major function is to prepare students for the Common Entrance Examinations to public secondary schools. Some are sponsored by traditional High Schools. The Secondary Schools have provisions similar to that of traditional High Schools, and prepare students for similar examinations.

West Indies College, a Seventh Day Adventist institution in Mandeville, is unique in that it offers programmes from pre-school to higher education levels. The Teacher Education Programme is accredited by the Joint Board of Teacher Education (JBTE) and provides teachers for public and private schools. Degree Programmes are offered in Business Education, Nursing Education, Secondary Education and Theology. The degrees are accredited by Andrews University in the United States.

Under the 1965 Education Act, Independent Schools were invited to apply for registration to denote whether or not their standards corresponded to national requirements. Of 385 schools which applied for registration between 1974 and 1980, 238 were successful, 21 became grant-aided, 13 were deferred, 34 withdrew and 53 failed to meet the requirements. When the schools are registered, they gain exemption from income tax, and government assistance is provided through in-service teacher training programmes and grants to those offering Vocational and Special Education.

Examinations

Examinations are used as a basis for selecting entrants to all levels of education beyond the Primary stage as well as to job opportunities. Some are local and internal to an institution. Others are external to the institution and may or may not be based overseas. The Common Entrance Examinations to the traditional secondary and technical schools are still given much prominence. The Grade Nine Achievement Test (GNAT) give late developers from All-Age Schools a second chance to enter secondary schools.

The Jamaica School Certificate (JSC) and the Secondary School Certificate (SSC) are local examinations operated by the Ministry of Education. The former is mainly taken by students from All-Age and New Secondary Schools as well as by private candidates. The SSC introduced since 1976 has been confined to students of New Secondary Schools. Its curriculum evolved from a philosophy that while having a core of academic subjects, students could have a strong bias towards vocational areas, hence its suitability to evaluate the wide range of vocational subjects in the New Secondary Schools.

The SSC differs from previous local examinations in that it carries two other components in addition to National Assessment which was the sole technique used in those examinations. These are School-based Assessment and Work Experience. School-based assessment includes tests and assignments administered by a school throughout the year. It contributes to 40% of the total marks. Work experience is provided in firms where the students' work is evaluated by the firms and monitored by the teachers.

Performance in the examination is evaluated in ranges 1 to 5. The range indicates the student's competence and possibilities in the subject areas. Ranges 5 and 4 indicate ability for continuing education at a higher level and so qualify students for entry to tertiary institutions. Range 3 indicates enough education for employment opportunities, while the other two ranges indicate minimum and very limited mastery of an area.

The General Certificate of Education and other external exams set by Overseas Examining Bodies for Secondary Schools are gradually being replaced by examinations set by the Caribbean Examination Council (CXC). The idea of a Caribbean Regional Exam was suggested by the Caribbean Association of Headmasters and Headmistresses in 1961, and the 1964 Caribbean Commonwealth Heads of Government Conference. Much discussion followed before the Caribbean Examination Council was set up in 1973 under the signatories of fifteen Caribbean countries. One has since withdrawn.

It was felt that a Caribbean exam could facilitate the formulation of courses more relevant to the needs of the area. With certificates being offered at both Basic and General Proficiency levels, a wider range of abilities is recorded. While Basic Proficiency level indicates completion of a secondary course in a specific subject and signifies readiness for employment, General Proficiency level indicates that the foundation has been laid for further studies. Performance levels are graded 1 to 5 with 1 being the highest.

Like the SSC, the CXC has provisions for continuing assessment in the forms of school-based assessment, project work, practical work and oral examinations. School-based assessment is used mainly for the practical areas. The CXC is a departure from former external exams taken by Secondary Schools, in that teachers are given an opportunity to participate in the final external evaluation of their students through their involvement in the formulation of syllabuses, and the setting and marking of examination questions.

Since the CXC is being developed as a replacement for the General Certificate of Education (GCE) and other overseas examinations at the Secondary level, parity would be sought. CXC levels one and two have been accepted as equivalent of Grades A to C in GCE 'O' levels, by the Joint ·Matriculation Board in England and by higher level institutions in the Caribbean.

Initially, some students entered for both GCE and CXC Examinations in the same subjects. Later, directives from the Ministry of Education stipulated that students sit the CXC in the subjects offered, so that schools only offer GCE in subjects that are not yet examined by the Caribbean Examination Council. The number of schools entering candidates for CXC Examinations increased from 281 in 1979 to 387 in 1981 and the number of candidates from 30,276 to 45,837. Beginning with five subjects in 1979, twenty-three were offered in 1982 and among them were practical areas such as Home Economics, Business Education and Industrial Arts. Another feature in the development of the examination has been provisions for the entry of private candidates. This will undoubtedly enhance the level of public support for the examination.

Tertiary Education

Under the *Education Thrust of the Seventies*, tertiary education was identified as an important area in which immediate action was necessary, and further development had to be made. In pursuit of this objective, new institutions have been established and former ones expanded. This expansion is in response to that at the Primary and Secondary levels of the education system. Changes in the curriculum at these levels have made changes in the curriculum at the tertiary level necessary.

Among the institutions offering tertiary education are Teachers' Colleges, CAST, Cultural Training Centre (CTC), the Vocational Development Training Institute, the former JSA replaced by the College of Agriculture, the G.C. Foster College of Physical Education, Community Colleges and West Indies College.

Teachers' Colleges

In 1973, the six teachers' colleges had an enrolment of 2100 and an output of 1015. It was projected that by 1978 the enrolment would reach 3500 and the output 1700. As a means of stimulating this expansion, the budgetary deficits of the colleges were removed and the allowances for students increased from $10 to $15 weekly.

The College of Arts, Science and Technology and the Jamaica School of Agriculture added teacher education departments, and a new teachers' college, Sam Sharpe, came on stream in 1976. Existing colleges have been extended in terms of additional classrooms, hostels, cafeteria and auditorium to meet the increased population. A variety of audio-visual equipment was supplied to the colleges through UNESCO. A new concept in the structure and organization of hostels at Mico and

140

Shortwood enabled students to take responsibility for part of their boarding arrangements and gain experience in self-reliance and social interdependence.

Although the enrolment in teacher education institutions for 1978 reached 5,718 and so surpassed the 1973 projection, the output of 1,618 fell short. Under the Rural Teacher Education Programme, another teachers' college, Passley Gardens in Portland, was opened in 1979. Its location in one of the island's leading agricultural centres and its proximity to an agricultural college, supports the assumption that its programme will be more rural-oriented than the other colleges.

All teachers' colleges offer a Primary Course. In addition some offer a Secondary and/or Pre-Primary Course. Colleges vary their offerings as teaching facilities and student intake permit. In the secondary course there is a slight degree of specialization. For instance, Industrial Arts and Double Option Science (Biology, Chemistry and Physics) are offered at Mico only. Library Science, a new area, has been introduced in some colleges to provide teacher-librarians for the secondary schools.

A new area of training in Special Education was made possible through the Netherlands Technical Assistance Programme. In 1976 facilities were provided at Mico College for training teachers of the handicapped (deaf, mentally retarded and physically handicapped). Experts from the Netherlands came to Jamaica to establish the programme. In the meantime Jamaicans were sent abroad on courses to equip them for teaching in the programme. As a further means of facilitating the development of Special Education, the Mico Child Assessment and Research in Education (CARE) Centre has been built and equipped to function as a remedial and diagnostic centre

141

for children with complex learning problems. The centre conducts courses for teachers, agency staff of special education institutions and parents of learning handicapped children. It carries out research into the nature and categories of handicapping and provides clinical practice for teachers of special education.

In another area of experimentation beginning September, 1973, Mico College was involved in a pilot project whereby some curriculum areas were reorganized to offer courses for six months. At the end of that period a final evaluation of the course was made. This approach, although used in other tertiary institutions such as CAST and JSA, was new to the teachers' colleges. By 1981, when the restructuring of the teachers' college curriculum started, it was extended to all teachers' colleges.

New courses have been formulated by the Boards of Studies which include personnel from the University, the teachers' colleges and the University. The Board of Teacher Education is the accrediting authority for teacher education in Jamaica. A major change in the restructuring of the teacher education programme has been the return to the three year intra-mural period of initial training. This proposal was made in the Five Year Plan (1978–83) and by a Conference on Teacher Education held in Jamaica in February, 1979. The return to the three year intra-mural programme was made on the presumption that the back-log of untrained teachers in the education system has been cleared. This is partly so since in the public system the percentage of trained teachers in the Pre-Primary (including grades 1 and 2) Sector stood at 81.4 in 1980. In the Primary Sector, it went from 48.8 in 1973 to 73.6 in 1980, and in the Secondary sector from 86.7 in 1973 to 92.2 in 1980. The In-Service-Teacher-Education Thrust

(ISTET), which produced 726 trained teachers between 1973 and 1979, has been phased out and the employment of Pre-trained teachers in the Primary Schools has been discontinued.

Beginning September, 1981, the colleges started a three year intra-mural diploma programme with minimum entry qualification of 4 GCE 'O' Levels or its CXC equivalent. A Preliminary Year has been introduced to enable students who fell below these qualifications to obtain the required number of 'O' Levels. Entrants with JSC or less than 3 'O' Levels are accepted for the Preliminary course. In some colleges, holders of 3 'O' Levels have been included in the Diploma Course and allowed to trail one 'O' level subject.

The introduction of the New Secondary Schools has brought a new dimension to the concept of secondary education in Jamaica. With a wide range of abilities among its students, more emphasis has to be placed on remedial and vocational courses as well as on guidance and career counselling. It would seem that teachers' colleges need to consider and respond to these changes in their teacher preparation programmes. Their adherence to preparation for teaching the traditional subjects may in part be due to their infrastructure and the cost of preparing teachers in the practical areas. The College of Arts, Science and Technology (CAST), Cultural Training Centre (CTC), G.C. Foster College of Physical Education, the Vocational Development Training Institute and the former JSA have been including teacher preparation in their programmes and meeting some of the needs of secondary schools.

College of Arts, Science and Technology
On account of its sensitivity to the needs of the society, the

143

number of courses offered at CAST almost doubled between 1973 and 1979. The level of offerings ranges from that of craftsman to the professional. In addition to the six departments mentioned in chapter VII, a Computer Centre has been established. It provides computer services for the college as well as offering courses to Data Processing trainees and for the British Computer Society Examination.

College of Arts, Science and Technology has secured the co-operation of both local and foreign organizations in making provisions to equip students with the skills needed in industry and commerce. Canadian International Development Agency (CIDA) has contributed in terms of building and training programmes to the development of Technical Teacher Education. An In-Service-Teacher-Education Programme has been offered since 1977 in association with the Canadian Teachers' Federation. Beginning in 1981, another in-service-programme, the Diploma in Education for Technical Teachers, has been started in association with the UWI School of Education and Huddersfield Polytechnic in England.

Over a six year period beginning 1974, a Telecommunications and Electronics Centre has been established and equipped through a cooperative venture involving the Government of Jamaica and United Nations Development Programme (UNDP) through the International Telecommunications Union (ITU). Jamaicans have been trained to operate the centre. Among the courses offered are modular and job-oriented ones for technicians. In developing its training programmes the centre aims at maintaining a good rapport with industrial companies.

The inclusion of Business Education in the curriculum of secondary schools has increased the demand for teaching personnel trained in this area. Furthermore, the significant number of CAST graduates who seek post-diploma studies abroad, as well as at the UWI, indicates the necessity for such provisions to be made locally in the areas of greatest need. In response to these demands CAST has started a B.Ed. (Post-Diploma) Degree Programme in Business Education on a part-time basis since July, 1982.

The Planning Technology Diploma Programme was developed with the aid of the Netherlands Government. Land Surveying, Medical Technology, Bilingual Secretary and Legal Secretary Certificates are just some of the courses offered since 1973. The Certificate Course in Institutional Management has been upgraded to the Diploma level and renamed Institutional Management and Food Science. A number of local accreditation bodies assess the internship students of CAST for purposes of registration, but CAST has been increasing its autonomy by providing internal assessment for several courses that were assessed by Overseas Examining Bodies.

A new concept in teaching methodology has been the introduction of a Work Study Programme of 30 hours on supervised projects in farming, building, construction, teaching, social work and student services for all first year students. This approach has been extended to involve students in the construction of some buildings at CAST, the utilization of the sewerage effluent on the College farm, and the experimention with the production of solar energy. Innovations in the curriculum of CAST, coupled with an expansive building programme, are indications of CAST's readiness for the proposed National Polytechnic repeatedly mentioned by government spokesmen over a long period.

Cultural Training Centre

The CTC came into existence in 1976 and is a complex housing the former Schools of Drama, Music, Dance and Art. The schools were formerly private institutions but in keeping with the policy of 'Free Education' are now under the management of the Institute of Jamaica. The Centre is administered by an academic board headed by a Director, and includes representatives from each school.

Among the aims of the Centre is that of fostering an awareness of how art and culture can contribute to the development of human resources in the Caribbean and other Third World countries. In keeping with this aim African and American Music has been introduced in the School of Music since 1975.

Each school operates full-time, part-time, evening and vacation courses, as well as a Junior Department which provides a laboratory for its teacher-training programme. Courses are for both professional and recreational purposes. The professional ones are offered to teachers, prospective artists, community leaders, craftsmen and artisans at both the Diploma and the Certificate levels. The Diploma is a 4 year course with entry level of 5 GCE 'O' Levels and includes the preparation of a thesis and an original production. The Certificate course is for 3 years with entry level of 3 GCE 'O' Levels or 7 JSC.

The courses for teachers are designed to enable graduates to meet the cultural needs of students as well as prepare those at the secondary level for job opportunities requiring applied arts and craft. The Ministry of Education recognises these courses, and accreditation by the JBTE is under discussion.

Although each school has a high degree of autonomy, in that each has its own Principal (Director), and Board of

Management, common courses are offered in Caribbean Studies, English and Communication and education theory. Elective courses, such as Anatomy, Theatre Arts and Traditional Folklore, designed by one school may be used by another, but each school has a curriculum specific to its area.

Vocational Development Training Institute
This institution was started at temporary locations in 1970 with the aid of funds from the UNDP and the International Labour Organization (ILO). Initially, it was to provide in-service-training for recruits from industrial and occupational fields. A World Bank loan provided classrooms after a permanent location was found. Overseas training for the Institute's staff was also procured through the World Bank.

As an arm of the National Industrial Training Board, the Institute acts as the certifying authority for the skills training programme of Vocational Instructors and Industrial Workers. It also guides the curricula of this programme and develops modular courses for industry on the basis of particular needs.

One of the problems that faced the New Secondary Schools at their inception was the inadequacy of teachers of vocational subjects. As there was no specific local institutions to provide these teachers, the VDTI recruited experienced tradesmen, and offered them courses to upgrade their skills and professional competence so that they could fill the vacancies in the schools. The programme is continuing, and includes Electrical, Automotive, Metal, Building, Construction and Wood trades. Basic Psychology, Methodology, Testing and Measurement, Communication Skills and Practical Teaching are included in the curriculum. It includes one year intra-mural studies plus one year on-the-job training.

Jamaica School of Agriculture (JSA)
For over 70 years, the JSA has been the island's premier institution in the provision of agricultural education. It has supplied recruits to industrial and commercial enterprises not only in Jamaica but in other countries as well. In recent years the demand for places at the school outstripped the available accommodation. For instance, 1782 candidates sat the entrance examinations for a possible 189 places in 1978. A teacher education pro-gramme was added to its curriculum in 1974, which provided agricultural science teachers for secondary schools. Beginning with an agricultural science option, Household Science was later added.

In 1975, a review and evaluation of the programme introduced in the school since 1969 was initiated. The authorities' anxiety to diversify further the school's programmes in an effort to maximize its services to the agricultural sector as well as develop economic self sufficiency was understandable. New projects were introduced to achieve these ends.

A Pre-Semester Programme in September, 1975 accommodated 160 First Years, and put the school's enrolment figures at a record 408 students including those due to graduate in December of that year. With the employment of a Physical Education tutor, scope was provided for the development of a physical education programme. An evening division was instituted at the school with offerings in various aspects of gardening. This was followed by GCE 'O' Level classes in the Science Subjects for people in the community.

As a part of a two-phased study sponsored by USAID, a team from the College of Agriculture, Florida University, together with their Jamaican counterparts, investigated the school's curriculum, organizational structure, placement, staff preparation, research activities, extension and community services. Following this study, the need to find means to decrease the school's dependence on government's subsidy was emphasized.

Efforts to improve conditions at the school led to the appointment of a committee to examine the two year course and consider its adequacy for the needs of the nation. Increasing emphasis on the practical areas included placement of students for one semester at an agricultural station. A project funded by the Norwegian government secured the expansion of the piggery and poultry farms, and the development of fisheries, crops and livestock projects were under consideration.

Despite efforts to make the school a viable entity, it was affected by the financial stringencies that hit the education system in the late 1970s. Conditions deteriorated so much that the intake of students in 1979/80 fell by 50% and classes did not resume in September, 1981. Second Year Students were transferred to Passley Gardens Secondary School where provisions were made to accommodate them. Dissension between the school authorities and the transferred students led to their expulsion. The repeal of the 1965 JSA Act was effected in January, 1982 and ended the existence of an historic institution.

But this did not bring an end to Agricultural Education at the Tertiary level as a new College of Agriculture sited at Passley Gardens opened in January, 1983 with a student population of 130. The incoming students included 14 of the former JSA students who have been cleared of involvement in the incidents which occasioned their expulsion. Initially, the new college will offer an Associate Degree in Agriculture. In addition to the Diploma Programmes, the JSA did offer an Associate Degree in Science and Agriculture. The policy-makers see the new college as the first move towards the establishment of the proposed polytechnic.

G. C. Foster College of Physical Education

This college was built and equipped by the Cuban Government under a Construction Agreement between the Cuban and Jamaican Governments. Jamaicans and Cubans worked jointly on the project. The College commenced operations in 1980 and has facilities for a variety of sports. It is under the jurisdiction of the Ministry of Youth and Sports, since one of its original objectives was to train coaches for that Ministry. However, its present function is that of preparing teachers of physical education, so it works in close collaboration with the Ministry of Education and the Joint Board of Teacher Education.

The entry qualifications are similar to those of teachers' colleges, and similar professional courses are offered over a three year period. In addition, students are required to choose two areas of study with particular reference to Physical Education, and one minor area from such subjects as Geography, English, Mathematics, Biology and Integrated Science. As teaching competence is required in both areas, it follows that students will offer them for teaching. The College serves as a centre for sporting activities and students are encouraged to share the benefits of their training with members of their community during vacation.

Community Colleges

The feasibility of operating Sixth Form subject groupings has been, and still is doubtful. A Working Party appointed in 1974 to study Sixth Form Education commented on the high failure rate in the 'A' level examinations, the narrowness of the curriculum, and absence of orientation towards community and national consciousness. Marketable skills were said to be scarce and some students described the course as boring.

In its recommendations, the Working Party stated the need for a broader curriculum to include general studies, and the consideration of Pre-vocational and vocational options as alternatives to the academic option addressed over the years. The fostering of community consciousness and involvement, as well as national and social awareness, should be made relevant. The Community College was suggested as the institution that would best convey the spirit of these recommendations and at the same time form a more appropriate sequel to the grades 10 and 11 programmes of secondary schools.

Knox and Excelsior Colleges, which operated programmes that could form the nucleus of a community college, operated as pilot schools. Based on the Community College idea, other schools in the vicinity of a community college lost their Sixth Forms to that institution.

Knox already had a Business Education Department that could be extended with funds from CIDA and the Public Welfare Foundation of Washington that were slated for the development of the College. Excelsior's development was included under a World Bank Scheme. Excelsior had Commercial and Teacher Education Departments, and later added a Nursing School, Business

Education Department and a course for Bilingual Secretaries. The provision whereby teacher education students did two subjects at GCE 'A' Level was discontinued when it was found difficult to achieve the desired results at 'A' Level. The programme is now confined to Teacher Education.

In September, 1975, Brown's Town and Montego Bay were added to the list of Community Colleges. At first, Montego Bay had no campus of its own, but operated as a co-operative venture involving three High Schools in Montego Bay with each offering some of the subjects. Community Colleges, in addition to offering Pre-university courses, are expected to cater to the needs of their community. So they offer both full-time and part-time (evening) courses in Business Education, Community Leadership and Library Science. Colleges vary in their offerings. For instance Brown's Town operates a JAMAL centre that is serviced by students of the College.

Links with other institutions and employment agencies in their areas are maintained. Excelsior offers a Business Education Certificate in conjunction with CAST. Brown's Town conducts courses for the staff of Kaiser Bauxite Company and operates as a centre for the School of Dance (CTC). Montego Bay prepares students for jobs in the tourist industry. In 1981 the enrolment of the 4 colleges stood at 1797. Business Education and Pre-University students totalled 583 and 510 students respectively, and are offered by all the Community Colleges.

University of the West Indies
Free education is as applicable to full-time first degree studies at the UWI as it is to courses in secondary and

152

tertiary institutions. Over a twenty year period beginning 1959, the number of students graduating with First Degrees increased from 107 to 1,361 plus another 625 with Certificates, Diploma and Higher Degrees.

A significant increase in registration has occurred in the areas of Agriculture, Arts, General Studies, Education and Social Sciences. Because of the scarcity of personnel in Physics, Mathematics, Chemistry and Geography, Scholarships and awards in these areas have increased at the expense of other areas. The School of Education has been restructured and now includes a Teaching Section, a Higher Degrees and Research Section and a Teachers' College Development Section. The last-mentioned has responsibility for the Certification of teachers, and in collaboration with the teachers' colleges develop their curricula.

In recent years, more attention is being paid to experimentation and research as the university addresses itself to the problems of the area. This is evidenced by a study of Jamaican Bauxite launched in 1976 in association with the International Atomic Energy Agency in Vienna and Metrimpex. The idea of a Challenge Exam became a reality when in 1977, for the first time, students from the Lesser Developed Caribbean territories sat examinations in the Part 1 Management Studies Programme without attending classes at UWI campus. They attended classes in their territories organised by the extra-mural department. This is a new technique to extend the services of the university to non-campus territories. The Institute of Management and Production in Jamaica has joined the non-campus territories in this programme.

Another experiment in 1976 assessed the value of the application of modern communications technology. Two satellites provided six hours weekly television and radio time for use through tele-conference by faculties, libraries, administration and course lecturing. The experience was shared by Mona and Cave Hill campuses. Following the evaluation of this experiment, consideration is being given to the development of two programmes. One is to be centred in Jamaica where facilities of a FM radio-based network within the existing broadcasting stations will be developed to promote teleconferencing between the School of Education and the Teachers' Colleges for the purposes of improving curricula, providing specialist teaching and dealing with common examination matters. The other proposal is to launch a UWI Pilot Project where tele-conferencing is used for education and public services including Outreach Programmes in the Caribbean.

A survey of Primary Schools in eight Caribbean territories was carried out by the Bureau of Latin America in 1977. It identified the need for improvement in the learning environment of Primary Schools and improved teaching methods through in-service-training. Resulting from this survey, a Primary Education Project sponsored by USAID and UWI was launched in 1980 to meet these needs. An aspect of this programme in which Jamaica has been involved is the Education Administration and Supervision Course for Principals. It includes vacation courses at UWI and visits to schools by resource personnel. Seminars are held with Principal and staff. The course aims at identifying curricular and administrative problems in the schools, and co-operating with Principals to find means of overcoming them.

The restructuring of the UWI, which has been under consideration since 1975, is now in its final stage.

Proposals have been made for each campus to have more autonomy in order to respond to the national needs of the host government. At the same time, the university will maintain central authorities for the maintenance of academic standards and the initiation of programmes beneficial to non-campus territories.

Special Education

A country whose goal is the development of an egalitarian society must make educational provisions available to children of all levels of ability. Unfortunately, the attention given to the education of the handicapped has not paralleled that given to normal children in Jamaica. For many years, the undermentioned voluntary agencies, with subsidies from the Ministry of Youth and Development and local parish councils, have been sponsoring education for the handicapped.

Handicap	Agency
Deaf and Hearing Impaired	Jamaica Association for the Deaf (JAFD)
Blind and Visually Handicapped	Salvation Army
Physically Handicapped	Polio Foundation Trust
Mentally Retarded	Jamaica Association for Mentally Handicapped

After the announcement of Free Education, government's participation in these programmes increased. An Education Officer with responsibility for Special Education was appointed, and a survey carried out to identify the enrolment and income of institutions offering special education.

The Schools for the Deaf include Lister Mair Gilbey (Papine) and St Christopher (Brown's Town). The former has Senior, Preparatory and Nursery Departments and is non-residential, while the latter accommodates the age group 4 to 10 years and is residential. Since 1978 the Preparatory Department of Lister Mair Gilbey has been renamed Danny Williams and recognized by the Ministry of Education as a Primary School for the deaf. A unit for the deaf has been accommodated at St. Hugh's Preparatory School too.

Provisions are made for the Mentally Retarded at the School of Hope and its branches and units throughout the island. Some units are attached to Primary and All-Age Schools while others are detached. The enrolment of this school inclusive of its units and branches went from 341 in 1973 to 890 in 1980. The Ministry of Education finances the programme through the principal school.

The Salvation Army School for the Blind provides facilities for the age group six to eighteen years. Between 1973 and 1980, the enrolment went from 112 to 131. Physically handicapped children are provided for at Hope Valley an integrated school as well as at a unit school for physically handicapped children.

In 1975 Education for the Handicapped was included in government's policy for the first time. This gave the sponsoring agencies an opportunity to upgrade their programmes. The hosting of the Caribbean Regional Conference on the Handicapped in Jamaica, and the involvement of the Ministry of Education in the conference was ample evidence of government's new attitude to the handicapped.

It was assistance from the Netherlands Government that gave the programme for the handicapped the financial stimulation and expert direction that it needed. Apart from the provision of teacher-training facilities, the Netherlands Government has established classrooms for the handicapped in several parishes, and expanded the residential facilities at St Christopher.

For a programme to be successful, planners must know the size of the population to be involved. To this end, a national survey sponsored by the Netherlands Government and the Jamaica Association for Learning Disabilities (JALD) was carried out among a sample of Primary, All-Age and Basic Schools. Its purpose was to assess the number of handicapped children in these institutions. With the assistance of USAID another survey attempted to estimate the number of handicapped children who were not enrolled in schools. A sample of communities throughout the island was used.

From the findings of the survey by the Netherlands Government and JALD, it was concluded that handicapped children could be taught in normal schools so long as special provisions with reference to curriculum and physical facilities were made for them. This idea is not new as special schools have been sending selected students to secondary and tertiary institutions through their Outreach Programmes.

Management and control of education

Since 1975, there has been no major changes in the structure of the Ministry of Education. But there has been decentralization in the activities of the Educational Operation, Construction and Maintenance Divisions. Regional Offices have been established in Mandeville, Montego Bay, Ocho Rios, Port Antonio and Kingston to take these services closer to the schools.

The Ministry of Education provides supporting services to facilitate the development of quality education in schools. The Education Broadcasting Service (EBS) is now a part of the multimedia centre which was established at Caenwood in 1976 with World Bank financing. The Education Broadcasting Service operates radio and television programmes for the benefit of Primary and Secondary Schools. It provides guides, manuals, charts, and workbooks in the various subject areas, advises teachers in the use of audio-visual aids, and services the audio-visual equipment given to schools.

In 1972 a USAID/GOJ Rural Education Sector Assessment Team identified the need for an education information system involving the Ministry of Education, the schools and public libraries as well as the provision of a statistical and data control centre. In response to this finding, an Education Development and Demonstration Centre has been established after a long delay. It includes an Education Information and Analysis Centre, Curriculum Materials Development Laboratory, a computer, conference and workshop facilities.

With respect to the welfare of school children, feeding grants from the Ministry of Education and gifts of food items from international and other national organizations provide cooked lunches for children in rural areas, while in the Corporate area, Nutrition Products Ltd, a government company, supplies children with a high protein snack. Each primary school child is supplied with one uniform per year. These provisions are intended to encourage better school attendance among economically disadvantaged children.

Although recommendations have been made for teachers' colleges to offer Supplementary courses in School Administration to prospective Principals and Senior teachers, this has not yet been implemented. But in addition to the training undertaken by USAID/UWI as part of the Primary Education Project, the Jamaica Teachers' Association (JTA) has been running seminars for these categories of teachers.

New policies regarding democratization and worker participation were introduced in public organizations in 1976. This brought about the restructuring of School Boards to include the Principal of the institutions and representatives of the academic, administrative, and ancillary staff, the student body, the past students' association, the Parent-Teachers' Association and the Community. The grant-aided denominational secondary school board has nineteen members, the public secondary fifteen, the denominational grant-aided primary nine, and the public primary, a maximum of eight. The Ministry of Education has the right to nominate the chairman for the Board of a public educational institution as well as one other member in the case of primary and All-Age schools, and three others in the case of Secondary Schools. In grant-aided denominational secondary schools, seven members including the chairman are appointed by the denomination while in the grant-aided denominational primary schools, the number of members appointed by the denomination is reduced to four.

The 1980 Education Regulations sanctioned the restructuring of School Boards, the recognition of Students' Councils, better leave facilities for teachers, arrangements for financing schools, and the monitoring of the appointment of pre-trained teachers among its new provisions.

This chapter has looked briefly at the institutions providing formal education that fall under the jurisdiction or influence of the Ministry of Education. But there are institutions that provide professional, technical, skilled and semi-skilled training as well as those providing non-formal education that cannot be accommodated here. The decline of the economy in the late 1970s accompanied by an increasing young population have resulted in a high rate of unemployment among school-leavers. Added to this, is the fact that many school-leavers possess no marketable skill. Priority must therefore, be given to projects which will ease this situation in any restructuring of the economy. It is for this reason that Human Employment and Resource Training (HEART) has been welcomed in 1982.

Under this programme, training and employment will be provided contemporaneously for a projected 12,000 young people annually who are not involved in formal education. This provision is for the 17–20 years age group who have 3 subjects in one of the local national or overseas examinations. The programme is a cooperative venture involving several Ministries of Government and the private sector. Employers in the private sector who participate in the scheme pay HEART employees $50.00 per week in lieu of a rebatable payroll tax of 3%.

Human Employment and Resource Training (HEART) includes a School Leavers' Programme where, in addition to skills learnt at the workplace, formal schooling will be available. Training is provided in building, garment manufacture, craft and agricultural skills. It is anticipated that this programme will fill the need for skilled workers in the society, as well as motivate the trainees to generate self-employment. The institution of this massive skills training programme, along with the eventual implementation of plans for revitalizing formal education, should lead to the full utilization of the human and material resources so essential for the political, social and economic reconstruction that is Jamaica's goal.

Bibliography

AAMM: Journal, 1944–64

Bailey, F. W.: 'History of the JUT Gleaner Co.' (1937)

Cundall, Frank: 'Mico College' The Gleaner Co. (1914)

CAST: Second Five Year Plan, 1979/80–1983/4

Department of Education, Jamaica: Annual Reports, 1914–55

D'Oyley, Vincent: 'Jamaica Development of Teacher Training Through the Agency of the Lady Mico Charity from 1835 to 1914' Department of Educational Research, Ontario College of Education, University of Toronto (1964)

D'Oyley, Vincent: 'The Development of Teacher Training in Jamaica, 1835–1913' unpublished Ph.D. thesis, University of Toronto (1963)

Easter, B. H. M. et al: 'A Plan for Post-Primary Education in Jamaica' Government Printer, Kingston (1946)

Evans, P. C. et al.: 'Report of the Committee on the Development of Teacher Training in Jamaica' Ministry of Education, Jamaica (December 1960)

Germanacos, C. L. et al: 'Report of the UNESCO Educational Planning Mission to Jamaica' UNESCO, Paris (1964)

Gordon, Shirley: 'A Century of West Indian Education' Longman (1963)

Handbook of Jamaica 1893–1950

Irvine, Sir James et al: 'Report of the West Indian Commission of the Committee on Higher Education in the Colonies' HMSO, London (1945)

Jamaica Government: 'The Gazette Supplement: A National Plan for Jamaica' Government Printer (1957)

Jamaica Government: 'Five Year Independence Plan, 1963–8' Government Printer, Kingston

Jamaica Government: 'Economic Survey, 1957–70' Government Printer, Kingston

Jamaica Union of Teachers: Annual Reports, 1916–54

Kandel, I. L.: 'Report of the Committee Appointed to Enquire Into the System of Secondary Education in Jamaica' Government Printer, Kingston (1943)

King, Ruby: 'The History of the Jamaica Schools Commission (1879–1911)' unpublished MA thesis, UWI (1972)

Laws of Jamaica 1892, 1914, 1926, 1953, 1956, 1963, 1965, 1980

Legislative Council Minutes

Lester Smith, W. O.: Penguin Education Books (1958)

Lomax, D. E.: 'The Education of Teachers in Britain' John Wiley & Sons (1973)

Lumb, C. F.: 'Report of the Committee of Inquiry into the System of Education in Jamaica' Government Printers, Kingston (1898)

Ministry of Education, Jamaica: Annual Reports, 1951–80

Ministry of Education, Jamaica: Code of Regulations, 1966 and 1980

Ministry of Education, Jamaica: Education Statistics, 1975–6, 1979–80

Ministry of Education, Jamaica: Five Year Plan, 1978–83

Ministry of Education, Jamaica: Education Thrust of the Seventies, May 1973

Ministry of Education and Social Welfare: 'A Review of the Development in Education and Social Welfare in Jamaica, 1944–54' Government Printer, Kingston (1945)

Murray, R. N.: 'Report in Depth of Primary Education in Jamaica' (1974)

Murray, R. N. and Gbedemah, G. L.: 'Foundations of Education in the Caribbean' Hodder and Stoughton, London (1983)

National Planning Agency: Economic and Social Survey, 1972–80

Piggott, H. H.: 'Report on Secondary Schools in Jamaica' Jamaica Schools Commission (1911)

Sterling, Rev. John: 'Report of Sterling to the British Government' (May 1835)

Whyte, M.: 'Struggle for Reform in the Teaching Profession of Jamaica Relating to Elementary School Teachers, 1918–30' unpublished MA thesis, UWI (1972)

Index

Advisory Group on Technical Education, 74
agricultural education, x, 14, 21, 24, 25, 28–9, 41, 43, 44, 53, 59, 63–75, 92, 107–8, 113–14, 132, 133–4, 135, 140, 142, 143, 148–50.
Association of Assistant Masters and Mistresses, 97–8, 101
Association of Headmasters and Headmistresses, 98–9, 101
Association of Teacher Training College Staff, 99–100, 101
Association of Teachers of Technical Institutions, 100
attendance at schools, 12, 17–20, 38, 124–5

Board of Education, 78–88
Board of Teacher Education, 52

Central Education Authority, 40, 87–93
churches and education, x, 3, 12–13, 16, 32, 34, 35, 37, 42–3, 47, 55–6, 76–8, 81, 85, 88, 94, 108, 136; see also missionaries; religion
College of Arts, Science and Technology, 53, 63, 140, 142, 143–5
Colonial Office, 14, 35, 68, 77, 79–80
Community Colleges, 112–14, 131, 140, 151–2
comprehensive high schools, 134; see also secondary education
compulsory education, 22, 23, 124–5
conditions of service of teachers, 94–104
Crown Colony administration, x–xi, 16–27, 33, 44, 77
Cultural Training Centre, 140, 143, 146–7
curriculum, 6, 9, 10, 11, 22–3, 24, 25, 26, 28–9, 32, 33, 34, 35–6, 37, 39, 40, 41, 43, 44, 45, 47–9, 51, 56–7, 63–5, 66, 67, 69, 73, 74, 98, 103, 110, 111–12, 117, 118, 120, 122–3, 125–7, 128, 131, 133, 135, 137, 140, 144–5, 147, 148, 149, 151

District School Boards, 80–4

early childhood education, 28–9, 110, 117–21; see also elementary education
Education Act (1965), 108, 124, 136

Education Thrust of the Seventies programme, xii, 109–14, 115–16, 129–30, 140
Educational Advisory Council, 40, 89–93
elementary education, x, 10–11, 14–30, 32, 39, 45, 66, 68–9, 84, 89, 100, 110, 136; see also early childhood education; primary education
emancipation, ix–x, 7–13, 15
English influence, ix, 1–6
Evans Committee, 52–3
examinations, 30, 34, 36, 38, 39–41, 45–6, 47, 52, 57, 58–9, 69, 70, 74, 77–8, 86, 99, 108–9, 128–9, 130, 133, 137–9, 145
external degrees, 59–60

finance and education, x–xii, 3, 4–5, 7–13, 14, 15, 16, 17–20, 21, 22, 28, 31–2, 33–3, 38, 40–1, 42, 49, 55, 58, 59, 60, 61, 70, 72, 76, 77, 85–6, 88, 91, 106, 117–19, 122–3, 130, 132, 149, 156
Five Year Plan for Education (1978–83), 116

G. C. Foster College of Physical Education, 140, 143, 150
grammar schools, 4–5, 107
Grant, Sir John Peter, 16, 21
grant-aided schools, 16–20, 21, 38, 40–1; see also finance

Hammond, S. A., 25–6, 39, 46, 48–9, 69, 98
health of children, 26–7; see also nutrition
higher education, 39, 51, 55–62, 65, 86, 99, 102, 108, 109–10, 140–55
Human Employment and Resource Training, 160–1

industrial education, 14–15, 21, 44, 63–75, 107–8, 135, 147–8; see also technical education; vocational education
independent schools, 135–7
in-service training, 47, 48, 51–4, 97, 103, 113, 121, 125–6, 137, 142–3, 144, 147–8
Irvine Committee on Higher Education (1944), 51, 61

Jamaica, passim

Jamaica College, 59
Jamaica High School, 33–4, 57–8, 67, 85–6
Jamaica Institute of Technology, 72, 73–4
Jamaica School of Agriculture, 53, 59, 63–4, 68–9, 92, 114, 140, 142, 143, 148–50
Jamaica Schools Commission, x, 33–41, 57–8, 68, 69, 84–6
Jamaica Teachers' Association, 99, 101–4, 116, 159
Jamaica Union of Teachers, 20, 24, 28, 46, 70, 94–7, 100, 101
Jamaican Assembly, 7–8, 13, 14, 16
junior secondary schools, 41, 107; see also secondary education
Joint Executives of Teachers' Associations, 101

Kandel Committee (1943), 39–40, 49, 50–1, 70–1, 73, 87, 88, 98, 107, 128
Kingston Technical High School, 70–2, 73, 100

Latrobe, 12–13
Legislative Committee (1926), 48, 83–4
London, University of, 59, 61
Lumb Commission (1898), 20, 22–3, 25, 34–5, 46–8, 67, 80, 83, 84, 89

management of education, 20, 76–93, 157–61
Marriot Mayhew Commission on Secondary Education (1933), 60
Mico Charity, 10–11, 43–4
Mico College, 46, 49, 50, 51, 58–9, 140–2
Minister of Education, 87–93
Ministry of Education, 103, 116, 117, 118, 120, 126, 137, 139, 146, 150, 157–61
Ministry of Education and Social Welfare, 87, 89–93
missionaries, ix–x, 5–6, 7–13, 21, 42–3, 76; see also churches; religion
model schools, 20–7, 44–5, 119
Moyne Commission, xi, 26–7, 28, 48–9, 61

Negro Education Grant, x, 7–13, 14, 32, 42, 44, 66, 76, 77
New Deal Programme, xii, 106–9, 115, 129
new secondary schools, 110–12, 131, 132, 133, 134–5, 137, 143, 147; see also secondary education
Normal Schools, 9, 10–11, 12, 13, 43–4, 45
nutrition and school children, 29; see also health

Parish School Boards, 80–4
payment by results system, 16–20, 21, 22, 25, 32, 66, 69, 77
Phillippo, Rev. James, 3–4, 55–6, 66
Piggott, Inspector, 35–7
post-primary education, 25, 40, 65, 69–70, 99, 102; see also secondary education
primary education, 9, 22, 34, 40, 49, 73, 99, 102, 106–8, 110, 113, 116–17, 119, 121–8, 129, 136, 140, 141, 154, 158; see also elementary education
pupil teacher system, 45–6

Queen's College, 56–9

religion and education, ix, 1–3, 5–6, 7–13, 15, 16, 78, 94; see also churches; missionaries
Rural Primary Education Project, 122–3

Rural Secondary Education Project, 133
Rural Teacher Education Programme, 141

salaries of teachers, 11, 12–13, 17–20, 96, 98, 100, 101, 103, 110, 121
school buildings, 9, 11–12, 27, 28, 37, 106, 121–3, 130, 132
secondary education, x–xii, 25, 29–30, 31–41, 49–51, 53–4, 55, 56, 57–8, 60, 65, 68–70, 73, 75, 84, 85, 86, 89, 97–9, 102, 106, 107, 108, 110–12, 113, 115, 128–37, 140, 141, 143, 147
Secondary Education Law (1914), 37
secondary high schools, 130–1; see also secondary education
Select Committee on Education, 24–5
Senior Schools, 29–30, 40, 107; see also secondary education
Shortwood College, 22, 46–7, 48, 49, 50, 51, 140–1
slavery, ix, 1–6, 7, 12; see also emancipation
Sligo, Governor, 65–6
Spanish influence, 1–6
special education, 141–2, 155–7
Sterling, Rev. John, 5–6, 7–12
Students' Loan Bureau, 109–10
Sunday Schools, 5, 10

teacher education, x, 6, 11, 20, 32, 33, 39, 41, 42–55, 66, 71, 84, 99–100, 103–4, 106–8, 113, 118–19, 120, 125, 136, 140–3, 147–8, 150, 151–2, 156; see also in-service training
teachers, quality of, 5, 11, 12–13, 36, 44–5, 48, 118, 120–1, 125
teachers' colleges, 140–3; see also teacher education
teachers' organization, 94–104
technical education, 41, 63–75, 131–2, 135
Technical Exploratory Committee (1949), 71
technical high schools, 131–2; see also secondary education; technical education
tertiary education see higher education
Thrust of the Seventies programme see Education Thrust of the Seventies programme

University College of the West Indies see West Indies, University College of the
University of London see London, University of
University of the West Indies see West Indies, University of the

Vestry Schools, 15
Vocational Development Training Institute, 140, 143, 147–8
vocational education, 63–75, 131–3, 151–2
vocational schools, 132–3

West Indies, x, 2, 5, 7, 13, 14, 26, 55, 58, 60–2, 67, 72, 99, 109
West Indies Federation, 105
West Indies, University College of the, xi, 61, 100
West Indies, University of the, 110, 152–5
Wood, Major, 23
work experience, 112, 132, 137–8; see also vocational education